Mum, Meet Mandy

How Ecstasy Changed My Life at Sixty

By Helen Brennan

Contents

Disclaimer

This book does not advocate or encourage the use of drugs of any kind. What it does, however, is advocate and encourage personal choice. Only you know the inner battles you face. I had battled mine for so long, I was defined as a person by them. When a light eventually showed itself, I was ready to come out of the dark. Did Mandy save me? No, but I saved myself by being humble enough to accept the introduction when it was offered, in the hope that it just might. My story, like yours, is a work in progress. Names have been changed to protect the privacy of the people involved, but all events are true. Any resemblance to persons living or dead is purely coincidental.

Dedications

I dedicate this book to anyone of any age who still hasn't found their tribe. To all the people I have met on my journey since Mandy. Some I still see, some I don't, but every one of them taught me something. My eldest daughter, for opening her heart and her life to me. I can never express my gratitude for her love and trust in doing so. My youngest daughter, for her casual acceptance of my journey, and her scathingly hilarious company in joining me on parts of it. And my son, for his rave stories, non-judgemental interest, and his unwavering care and concern for my well-being. Last, but not least, my husband. He listens, debates, and tries to understand my ever-changing moods and ideas with endless patience, cups of tea, and tech support. Without him, it would all be so much harder.

EVERYTHING STARTS SOMEWHERE

Up popped a video of a cat playing ping-pong, then a detailed picture of someone's lunch yesterday. Adverts for multivitamins. I scrolled through Facebook on autopilot, my mind was blank and my cup of tea going cold. Suddenly my phone rang, making me jump.

"Hiiii!!"

It was my eldest daughter, Melanie.

"Mum, I've been thinking." (She was always thinking, WE were always thinking, and often my thought was that we really shouldn't) "You know you're sixty soon?"

Did I know? Next year would be the big six-O – a fortnight after Melanie's birthday when she would be forty-three.

"Well," she continued, "I think with it being an important birthday and near mine, we should do something to celebrate together. What do you think?"

"Sixty?" I barked into the phone. "What mad words are you spouting? I don't even know what sixty means and I refuse to be it, so there!"

I was half-serious. Sixty meant nothing to me and had no relation to how I looked or felt. Sixty was for bus passes. Sixty was for age-related benefits, knit-and-natter groups at the local Tech, and beige waterfall cardigans. Sixty was NOT for me.

We chatted a little while longer about this and that, and then Melanie had to take my little grandson, Louis, to school. I was tipping the cold tea down the sink as the kettle re-boiled when my phone beeped again. It was a video message from Melanie, with the subject, 'How about we do this?' Back on the sofa with my fresh cuppa, I pressed play. Melanie's kitchen came into view. I nearly spat the tea all over the floor as I watched, captivated.

"So, this is what I was thinking." She stepped back to get the camera angle right and began what I can only describe as an epileptic doing 'Simon Says Skip' (I am sincerely sorry if you have epilepsy or know anyone who has. It must be terrible, but I haven't, and I don't, and I'm just saying it as I saw it).

"What the hell," I mouthed silently, "is she doing?" Melanie bobbed and jigged around her kitchen.

"This is Running Man," she said as she lifted one knee, sliding the other foot back on her floor tiles. Indeed, she looked exactly like a person trying to run on ice. "This," she said with a grin, changing to what resembled an over-enthusiastic Scottish jig, "is quite hard to do, but with a bit of practice…"

Quite hard!?

The show continued through another seven or eight crazy flurries of footwork before her face zoomed into a close-up. She beamed, out of breath. "So, I reckon if we both learn the Rave Shuffle (this trial-by-dance move had a name apparently), we can surprise everyone by doing it together if we go out for our birthdays. Byeeeee!" She blew a kiss, and the screen went blank. 'Surprise' wasn't the word.

I sagged back on my cushion. Melanie surely could not be serious, and yet it looked good, it looked fun, and with a LOT of practice, almost possible. I idly loaded Facebook again and began scrolling to see what I'd missed in the past thirty minutes. Almost immediately, there was an advert for a savings plan for the over fifty-fives. They say social media listens to you, but this was ridiculous. I paused, then with the masochistic curiosity born of my conversation with Melanie, I pressed, 'see more'. I scrolled through the application form until I got to the obligatory age boxes.

20–35

35–50

50–65

65–75

75+

It hit me that my whole life had been spent sliding further down the scroll boxes until I hovered two boxes away from the plus sign. The companies couldn't be bothered to add another box after seventy-five. Well, you'd either be dead or you wouldn't be saving a right lot before you were, eh?

I heard the gate clang next door and turned to look out of the window. Mrs Cartwright was just off shopping. I caught sight of her grey bob as her head disappeared around the corner. She and her hubby were in their mid-sixties, and we often saw their grandchildren in the garden in the summer. Sometimes, we chatted over the fence for a few moments as we were passing. She had a lot of trouble with her veins and had to wear a bandage around her calf. It smelled strongly of liniment, and she had to change it every night before bed. Not that it put her hubby, Frank, off. She joked that he was way past that kind of palaver, anyway. I never heard her swear, Mrs Cartwright. She was a lovely lady.

I glanced at the time on my watch. I had better get a move on. Hurrying out of my back door, I strode up the seventy-two (I've counted many times) steps to my converted garage and flicked the lights and water heater on. I work as a dog groomer in the mornings and a walker in the afternoons. Before you go *"Awwwwww",* I'll tell you, it's a messy, dirty job. With only a few exceptions, most dogs are knob-heads. Take Pepsi the Springer Spaniel, for example. Like the old fingers-in-warm-water trick, the slightest trickle of tepid water touches his tail end – and he hunkers down for a dump. Until you've scraped dog poo and the resulting hot, lumpy gravy out of a plughole, you haven't known nausea. The stench is enough to scald your retinas.

I flicked through my paperwork and checked the bookings. Five minutes until Pepsi the pooper was due to arrive. As I sat down to wait, I mused. Mrs Cartwright… me… old Frank… dodgy veins… me again… mid-sixties… savings plans…

Grinning to myself, I swiped across my phone screen and texted a quick reply to Melanie,

"That's a bloody ACE idea! Love it! Let's do it!"

I am NOT an age in a box! Not anymore. But it wasn't always like that though, so let us begin…

Once upon a time in a kitchen up north… Hang on. Once? Did I say 'once?' Nope, this is the real world, and what I felt wasn't once. It was every single day. Okay, let's start again. Hello everyone, I'm Helen; I'm sixty, and I'm a recreational drug user.

ONE IS ONE

Have you ever felt so lonely, so empty, that you wept as though you would never stop? I remember that day as if it were yesterday. In a way, it almost was. It was in 2020 when the COVID pandemic was about to lock down the lives of millions of people that my life, and that of my husband Josh, changed forever. Forever – how cliched does that sound? But it did, and from that day there was no going back because that's the day we became destined to meet Mandy. I had no idea what or who Mandy was, and maybe you don't either. Well, 'Mandy' is the name on the street for the drug MDMA, which is the active ingredient in ecstasy tablets or 'E's. In America, it's better known as 'Molly'. If you'd told me that a few years ago, I would have been unable to hide my dismissal and disapproval. But hey! Things change, right?

There wasn't a sudden shudder or crack in my otherwise contented conveyor belt of middle life. It was years in the coming – years beginning almost from birth. If you believe that every aspect of your life is predestined, that all your experiences have worked toward the current moment, then mine was on a crash-hug with Mandy.

My husband, lovely, younger, and supportive (but often confused and at a loss), Josh, was perched on our kitchen worktop. He had taken refuge there from my seemingly irrational tears and dramatic ramblings. They always ended with the obsessive desire to latch onto strangers, or anyone at all who would suffice as a companion. I would end with the desperate pleading, "I need a friend". Poor Josh, he'd heard it all before, and could only partly relate. Although he didn't have close friends either, he simply didn't feel the same way. His needs were different, but our journey together now is the same.

Someone once asked me, if you could have one wish that wasn't based around world peace or endless cash, what would it be? I'm pretty sure if pressed, that I'd wish for something like a farm in the country. My genuine wish is a little more unrealistic than that – especially now. I wish for one night, just one, with my mum, on Mandy. I want one night to know her, to feel and connect with her; the person no one, not even my dad, I suspect, has ever seen. I know that the medicine Mandy could offer would release her, my dad, my sister, and me from a lifetime of bitterness, sadness, and confusion that we have all suffered on various levels. Mandy could lift her and pull us together in an emotional embrace that otherwise would never exist. Mandy would help me forgive, and to reach out with the purest of love, to a heart that never truly learned what love is. Mum is knocking on for eighty-six years old, so now it's too late.

I try to believe it was a generational failing. Parents then weren't as emotionally demonstrative toward their children as they are now, and physical expressions of love simply weren't as common back then. Mandy prompted me to accept my parents back into my life after almost ten years of estrangement when, during COVID, my mum messaged me asking to 'start again'. I was very wary, and I'm certain the reason behind the message was a realisation that they are both now getting old and will need my sister and me one day. Does that sound cynical? Yes, but then, I know my parents. My dad recently had a fall and is now very frail since COVID put a stop to their hobby of sequence dancing or any other activities, so my mum will certainly have been given pause for thought. As a non-driver, she relies completely on my dad to get around. I did not wish to, and will not start again, in the same roles as before. I allow myself and them a relationship where I simply no longer want or expect anything from them. I will be there for them as their daughter and next of kin. I can spend an afternoon drinking tea and letting them talk about themselves, as they have no interest in my life or anyone else's. I can give them both a hug and see them off with a "love you!" It's the best we can all do under the circumstances. Had I not been introduced to Mandy; I would have never had a relationship of any kind with them again. Mandy re-opened my heart.

My parents were born before the Second World War, and things were different back then. It was tougher, in so many ways that our generation and my grandchildren's generation will never understand – and why should they? We constantly berate the younger generation for not appreciating the hardships that went before them, but do *we*? We read books, listen to anecdotal evidence, and watch movies. We collect antiques – as if by doing so we can buy a little of the life lived at the time these things were made, but we neither understand nor feel the feelings. We simply replicate them as best we can. That's what my parents, particularly my mum did; she learned to replicate feelings. I was born in 1962, the eldest of two sisters. My sister Katy was born two years later. She's blonde, has a great sense of humour, is fiercely independent, and is the opposite of me. Brunette and needy, I'm the troublesome one. I believe my parents did what they were supposed to do. I also believe they would have been so much happier had they never had children, but again, times were different – and that wasn't a thought, much less an option. Speaking of myself and Katy, Mum told us many times, "Our lives didn't start until you two left home."

The eldest of three sisters in a poor Southern Mining town, I remember my mum saying of my grandad, "He only became a miner to get free coal. He was hardly ever at work, but we got free coal for life." This sums up everything about my mum. She never wanted to be a 'scratter' – poor and with no self-respect, but she viewed her parents as guilty of both. Nobody has any positive attributes. She sees the worst in everybody. My mum as a teenager was beautiful. Photographs show her with a rich brown waist-length ponytail, a circle skirt, and ankle socks, as was the fashion of the time. She still has a fantastic figure even now. Back then though, my aunt remembers her as impatient, and dismissive of others in her desire to better herself. My mother had little empathy for people even then. She had a friend who lived a few doors down, Margaret, who sadly got cancer in her very early twenties. She was Mum's best friend, but as cancer ravaged her body, killing her bit by bit, Mum dropped contact entirely. Much later, when my parents were in their late seventies, their neighbour (who regularly invited them around for meals and card games – and they went) became terminally ill and was housebound. I asked Mum how he was.

"I don't know," she said. "We haven't seen him."

"Well, why don't you pop around?" I suggested. "It's nice to show you care. I'm sure they'd appreciate it."

"I don't think so," she halted the conversation. "It's not like we were friends or anything."

When he died, his wife was alone with no family to visit. Mum never spoke to her again.

I have many memories of my maternal grandparents – most of them as lazy, uncaring, and what we used to call 'common people'. The memories are a combination of images of them in my mind, but the words are ones I heard from my mum. Nanan and Grandad lived with Mum's unmarried younger sister and her small son. They lived on a rough estate, in a half-brick council house with pebble-dashing and a corrugated tin roof. The house was built after the war to help solve the housing shortage. Mum and Dad would joke about the wheels being stolen from our car if it was parked outside their house for too long. Katy and I were afraid to go into the 'best room', as on top of a dark wooden bureau, was a statue of Christ baring his chest to show his raw and bleeding heart. This image cowed and terrified us, and we would hurry past, clinging to Mum's coat. The toilet was an adjoining brick outhouse; pitch black inside, scary and freezing. It had no lighting and had newspaper on a string to wipe your bum. Mum told me and Katy that my granddad drowned kittens in a bucket there when she was a child.

Thinking back, it was obvious from our very first understanding of adult conversations that my mum was ashamed of her parents and her roots in the town. She met my dad, a handsome (and he is still), auburn-haired young man, when he was visiting neighbours on Nanan and Grandad's street. Dad was in the Royal Air Force. Photographs show him looking dashing and proud in his uniform, with a kindly smile and twinkling eyes for the camera. When they married, Mum vowed to change her accent and her clothes, and discard everything that connected her to her past. She and my dad moved to the small village where my dad was born and where I live now, but back then, it wasn't an affluent tourist area as it is today. It was bleak, and locals were very 'cliquey' about outsiders moving in. Mum was an outsider with no intention of fitting in. She was able to block out people and feelings, and it was this ability that underlined our whole family dynamic and future relationships. My mum's parents had very little money, and a charade that played itself out every time we visited (two or three times a year) was that of the cake with the silver balls.

Upon preparing to go home, my Nanan would give my mum and dad a gift of a homemade cake, with thick white royal icing, and decorated with silver candied balls. I remember the cakes well. They would be burned black on the outside, rock hard on the inside, and the silver balls would chip teeth and cut your gums if you ate them. With shouts of "Bye!!!! Come again!" we would set off home in the dark, bumping over the railway tracks as we left the outskirts of their estate. Dad would drive us back to our twee little village, twenty-five miles away. We had a routine upon arriving home. Dad would park the car outside our house, and we'd all clamber out. Dad would be first down the path, and as he passed, he would lift the bin lid. Katy and I would be following behind and, bringing up the rear, Mum would tip the cake into the bin before going into the house.

A million times over the years, Katy and I have wondered how much of our mum and her relationship with us was tainted and predetermined by her upbringing. Sex was never spoken of in our house, and I never recall seeing my parents hold hands, kiss, or show any physical affection toward one another. They never swore and even as an adult, I wouldn't dream of doing so myself in their company. Alcohol was a similar no-no, although there was a bottle of ginger wine secreted away in my dad's wardrobe – medicinal, you understand (and it wasn't that secret, because Katy and I found it whilst searching for our Christmas presents). We never saw our parents drink, even on special occasions. The story my mum tells is that not long after they were married, Dad went on a works' do with a few of his colleagues. He got so drunk that when he got home, he couldn't get down the drive in a straight line. He tripped over a stone flag and fell. Mum came out to discover him laughing and rolling about on the lawn. She stood stock-still, staring at the spectacle before her.

"Get up, you stupid man!" she hissed, glancing around to see if this exhibition had been viewed by any of the neighbours. Shame-faced, Dad half slunk, half wobbled into the house. Mum proudly told us he never dared to get drunk again. He never went out with friends again either.

Mum has had nothing at all good to say about her parents or sisters to this day. It's clear to us as adults that they thought she looked down on them when she moved away and married our dad. In fairness, though, I've never seen another buffet that has boasted bread and dripping, Jaffa cakes, and malt loaf with margarine displayed next to the wedding cake, as I did at my cousin's wedding.

Of course, we benefited as children from her turning her back on her past and making something of herself. She often said that if we had been brought up with the broad dialect of her hometown, we would have been bullied mercilessly in school. That was the way back then, with 'comers in'. Unfortunately, Mum didn't get to know anyone in her new community, as she was determined that no one find out where she came from. She actively shunned neighbours and people who had the potential to become real friends. She never invited people in, and still to this day won't put herself out for anyone – family included. I don't believe Mum has ever done anything simply to make someone else smile. She believed, and still believes, that "The less people know, the less they can talk about". There's no denying the accuracy of that statement, but I think Mum would have been a different person had she had a friend to talk to. She had some setbacks, as we all do, but she let them taint her view of people. When faced with similar setbacks, I, however, became embarrassingly more determined to open up to anyone who showed an interest, and many who didn't.

Mum always worked in the little town she hated. She always had a job, so differed from her parents in that respect, and Katy and I inherited a strong work ethic. We had everything we physically needed to live comfortably. My dad worked hard as a joiner and builder, and we were the 'posh' side of the family to my grandparents, but what we needed most were love and cuddles. There is little doubt that Mum's parents were correct in their assessment of the situation. Her sense of shame and embarrassment in her background cost both her and us dearly in the years to come. She became cold and hard, her manner of speech aggressive and snappy. She must now be concerned about how she will cope when my dad goes. He is much weaker now, and Mum is going to need us if anything happens to him. I don't doubt that she will expect us to be there for her (and we will).

Only last year, during a rare moment, I was able to tell her how I felt. Mum said she blamed *her* parents for her inability to demonstrate love, as they weren't loving either. Sober, but calmed and changed by the liberation and self-worth Mandy has given me, I was able to respond with, "Mum, I never had to learn from anyone how to love my children. It was just there."

By the way she looked at me, I detected her inability to understand what I was saying. When I recounted that there wasn't one memory, one photograph of her holding or hugging me, even as a baby, I could see it still didn't register as important. I tell a lie; there is one photograph of Mum looking super glamorous, in the style of the young Queen

Elizabeth (Katy and I call it the 'Her Majesty at Home' photo). I am around two or three and even then, she is holding me toward the camera at full arm's length. Some might say she was proud and showing me off, but I'm not so sure.

I became a rebel – a horrible, lying, stealing child. I would do anything for attention. Understandably, some people would say, 'Why would you want negative attention and punishment? I don't believe that!' Of course, they don't. Why would they? It makes no sense at all, but I lived it. I was an absolute nuisance. I was good at drawing, but not quite good enough. I wanted my parents to be proud of me, so I traced until I was caught and punished. Because I had no friends at junior school, I was desperate for someone to like me. I decided to steal biscuits and buns from home to give to the other girls. I would sneak into the pantry and grab whatever biscuits were closest and shove them into my schoolbag. I was caught and my parents were called in to see the headmaster about my behaviour. Of course, once back at home, my parents punished me for this misdemeanour by not letting me play out or being sent to bed without any tea. I told my schoolteachers that my parents had glamorous jobs and were famous people. I pretended to be ill so they would send me home. This stunt worked, but upon arrival home, cuddles still eluded me. My parents were quick on the ball to shout and punish these transgressions, but hugs didn't exist no matter how much Katy or I were hurting.

My parents had a budgerigar called Minty. In the evening, he would be allowed out of his cage to fly freely around the living room, and one day he landed on my head and crapped on me. Of course, there were gales of laughter as I picked the slimy poop from my hair. This started what I can only now understand as a child's form of self-harming. I was paranoid that there was still budgie poo in my hair and that the children at school would laugh at me. I took to smoothing my hair with my fingers until I found a rough bit (which I now know was simply the ends of my hair). I would tie a knot in the hair and forcibly rip it out. This went on for months, and the children at school did laugh, but only because I looked like Worzel Gummidge. Even the local shopkeeper took to calling me 'Tatty Head'. My habit only stopped when Mum threatened to make me wear woolly mittens to school. Poor Katy was ignored as I became the focus of my parents' attention, at last.

One year, Katy and I, at seven and nine years old, made a Mother's Day card for our mum. We painstakingly cut out and stuck magazine pictures and dried flowers on the card, making a mess but done as carefully as small children can. The day before Mother's Day, we were excited to spot a gold cardboard box on the floor by a bin outside – one of those flat ones for posh cards. It was clean and fit our homemade work of art perfectly. Proud as punch, we gave it to Mum in bed the next morning. We hopped from foot to foot with excitement, grinning at each other, and her, anticipating how pleased she would be. Wrong again. She took one look at the box and began to yell about wasting money on posh cards. This was before she had even opened the box. The shouting went on and on. I have no memory of what she said when she finally did open it. Katy and I were crying too much to listen.

Similar scenarios played out throughout my school life. I believed that if I gifted people things, they would like me. I gave other children my toys so they would play with me. If I had nothing to give, I would draw pictures for their homework or act like the village idiot, so they'd think I was funny enough to spend time with. One day I was talking to a girl in primary school who was popular and had lots of friends. She was telling me about her Sindy dolls and how she wanted the Sindy doll bed for Christmas. I'd seen the bed in the catalogue my parents used to buy things from. I told her I'd get her one and bring it to school. With the typical naivety of a young child, I went home and crafted my own version of a Sindy bed, using cereal boxes and tape. I proudly took it to school the next day, put it on her desk, and waited with nervous excitement and hope. When the girl came in and saw it, she laughed at me and tore the cereal boxes up in front of me. All the other girls were pointing at me and laughing, too. Even now I can still feel the hot shame of that moment, and I carried that shame for many years until not so long ago. I bumped into the girl in question in the street, now in her late fifties. In an attempt to finally exorcise the memory, I tentatively referred to this 'funny and embarrassing tale of things kids do', only for her to admit that "I honestly can't remember it, sorry."

Katy and I were never allowed friends in the house like other children. Of course, we were invited to friends' houses and so played there in the school holidays. We got on with their parents as we were polite and didn't cause any trouble, so they never minded us hanging around. However, the pattern of our lives for many years to come became one of trying to please our own parents. On every special occasion when we were older, we'd get together and wrack our brains and confer over what we could buy or organise to make our parents happy on their birthdays. The list was endless: helicopter rides, meals out, coach trips, theatre shows with champagne and chocolates, flowers delivered, and handmade gifts. It went on and on, but then stopped. Our joint supply of love and effort had been exhausted. Neither of us could do it anymore, constantly trying to fill a leaking well that would never quench our collective thirst. We'd given up. I still have a scrap of paper with part of a poem written on it in a childish scrawl. It was probably from one of the many times Katy and I had been sent to our room for being troublesome. I would have been about six or seven when I wrote it.

"Mum's mad, she's always mad,

shout, shout, mad, mad."

Like most childhoods, it wasn't all bad. My dad is a gentle, funny guy and tried hard to do things with us, often in the face of her disapproval. He is utterly dominated by Mum and will do anything to keep the peace and avoid her temper. When she's in that kind of mood, she will usually shout at and belittle him, regardless of who is there. Katy and I have often remonstrated with Mum about treating him this way, but learned quickly that he will turn on us and back her up anyway. Nothing must upset Mum! Dad wanted to get Katy and me a pet when we were small and one day he came home from work with two rabbits in a cardboard box. He was so pleased; he was going to make a hutch and they were going to live in the garden. I don't remember the rabbits at all. They went straight back in the box and disappeared the next day, back to whence they came. Mum filled us in years later.

"Your stupid dad got a boy and a girl! Can you imagine if we'd kept them? We'd have been overrun with rabbits!"

She had a fair point, of course, but this is the way she spoke of my dad and still does. I can't count the number of times we've stepped in and asked her not to talk to him so disrespectfully. To no avail, she carries on and he just smiles and shrugs. Using his skills as a joiner, Dad handmade a couple of wooden doll houses for Katy and me. They weighed a tonne, but had staircases and gardens. They were beautiful, and I decorated the walls with cut-out paper and made little pictures to hang up in the living room. It was Dad who went horse riding with me on holiday, as he knew I loved horses. He had never ridden a horse in his life before then. Thinking back, I bet us girls provided him with the opportunity to try quite a few fun things Mum would never have approved of. He laughed like a drain as my horse wandered off back to the stables for its tea, with me hanging red-faced around its neck. He was the one who went on all the crazy white-knuckle rides with Katy and me on our yearly holidays to Butlins Holiday Camps. Struck rigid with terror, we three would be chucked about at breakneck speed on rusting and creaking machines emblazoned with slogans such as 'Scream to Go Faster' and 'Fastest Fear Flume Ever', while Mum shielded her eyes from the sun on the ground. We loved Butlins. We would spend hours on end in the penny arcades looking around on the floor and in the money trays of the machines for spare coins once we'd spent up. There was a machine shaped like a flying saucer that you'd slot coins into the top of. They'd run down a chute and fall into randomly placed pockets inside that were designed to look like the craters on a planet. Once a crater was full of coins, the weight would cause it to drop, and you won the coins. Of course, if you were sneaky enough to avoid the arcade owner, the bigger kids would lift the edge of the machine a few inches. They'd then let it drop with a bang and run like the clappers, leaving all the little kids to clean up. The resulting shudder caused the craters to tip their booty. To this day I do not know what came over Mum, but on one visit to the arcade, she had a swift scan around, backed up to the machine, lifted and dropped it! The almighty crash, jangling of falling coins, and whooping kids, alerted all and sundry to the fray. As we backed away like burglars melting into the night, the arcade owner appeared, looking angry.

"Excuse me, Madam," he snapped at her in exasperation, "please don't bang the machines. We have enough trouble here with the children."

Nice one, Mum!

My parents gave Katy and me spending money each day at Butlins, and we decided we wanted to take back a small gift for Dad's mum, Grandma Ida. We couldn't agree on which pottery seahorse thermometer to buy – the luminous green or the luminous red. Both were utter monstrosities and typical of the seaside tat that was so popular at the time, but we were sure Grandma would love one. After ages and much cajoling and threatening no time for ice cream if we didn't hurry, we chose a beautiful emerald green one and handed our precious pennies over. We clutched our tissue-wrapped parcel and set off for the Waltzers. Quite rightly, Mum figured that delicate pottery in the hands of kids being thrown around at remarkable velocity had little chance of making it home in one piece. She ignored our whining and pleading to the contrary and had us hand it over to our dad to take safely back to the chalet. Much later, tired and hungry, we made our way back, and over tea, we inspected our purchases. Katy and I again marvelled at how pleased Grandma Ida would be with her apple-red seahorse.

"Red? A what? Red? Surely, we got the green one?"

"No," said Dad firmly. "You got the red one, you whined and changed your minds about it that many times you've forgotten."

A few years later, Dad, smirking, admitted that on the way back to the chalet he'd dropped the green seahorse and broken it. Too embarrassed to admit it after all the accusations that we couldn't be trusted to keep it safe, he hot-footed it back to the stall to buy a replacement, only to find that the green ones were all sold out. Bless him. Grandma Ida was never any the wiser and loved her red seahorse. It's still a memory that makes us smile even now.

TEENAGE DIRTBAG

At fourteen, I was a rebellious and unpleasant teenager. My relationship with my parents had become a constant battle of wills based on mutual dislike and indifference. I learned quickly that my looks, flirtatiousness, and decent bust size could get me all the 'love' I needed. At fourteen, I was sleeping with my first boyfriend, Rich, to whom I lost my virginity in an old cowshed. It stunk and was dirty, but to me, it was the epitome of romance. Sneaking home that night with blood on my new dark green skirt, I felt like a real woman.

I met Rich when I was on my paper round. Getting up at the crack of dawn, I would walk the half mile down to the paper shop in the village. A few moments later, laden down with newspapers and magazines, I'd deliver them along a circular route that took me past all the posh houses and farmland and back home. I would see Rich as I passed his house each morning, and although he never spoke, I often caught him watching me as I passed. He looked like Rod Stewart, who was a favourite teenage heartthrob of the 1970s, and a bad boy. Rich was four years older than me; he had a motorbike and a job. So, when one day he took the opportunity to tell me his neighbour was away for the weekend, so they wouldn't need a paper, I spent a few moments chatting with him. A few days later, he asked if I fancied going to a local church disco. Did I?! I couldn't say yes fast enough.

I felt so grown up going on my first date. Dressed in my best flared jeans, I smeared on some blue crème eyeshadow I'd bought from Woolworths and went to meet him. Rich had refused to call for me and asked me to meet him at the end of the road instead. Off we went, me trotting alongside him. Rich wouldn't hold my hand, but that was alright too. Maybe he was shy? He didn't want to dance either; he spent all night at the bar while I just stood there like a spare part. I was late home and ended up in trouble with Mum and Dad because Rich had ended up punching some lad over an argument about his ex, but I thought he was wonderful. We never went to discos again, and we never went on another date after that. Rich treated me like dirt, but I was besotted with him and simply ignored all the warning signs. We had sex every time we met up. He spent time with me and later introduced me to his mates, who laughed because I had a paper round and adored him so much. He *must* love me, surely?

Tolerating any indignities for attention, I bought Rich gifts with my paltry wage from my paper round and fawned on his every word. I wrote poems about him and imagined every soppy pop song was written for us. Each had meaning solely for me and him. He loved me, even though he pushed me around and called me names. I was immediately popular because I had an older boyfriend, or so I thought. My teachers thought I was a pain in the arse, and my peers likely thought I was the class bike. I wasn't fashionable enough to be friends with the popular girls. Although Mum and Dad always owned their own house and were never short of money, Mum reverted to her own childhood when she had very little and would take Katy and me to try on second-hand clothes that were advertised in the free newspaper in our village. This meant that all my clothes were in danger of being recognised at school by their previous owners and were going out of fashion by the time I got them. Unfortunately, this meant I quickly became a target for bullies. The only friends I had were two other girls who also had older boyfriends, bunked off school with me, and drank underage in the village pub. They were happy to be friends with me if I did what they wanted and participated in whatever mischief they got up to. The landlord of the pub was an alcoholic and too pissed to know we were there. Locals would go behind the bar and help themselves to the spirits when he fell into a drunken stupor, and we'd steal records from the back of the jukebox where it was broken.

There were only eight or nine records left out of the one hundred to choose from by the time we were done. Customers lost a lot of ten-pence pieces in that jukebox!

It was when Rich broke up with me for a few weeks when I was fifteen that I discovered drugs for the first time. I was heartbroken. Our Katy hung around with some of the other pub kids, and they would smoke weed and eat the magic mushrooms that grew locally. Our village was a haven for the real hippies and the seventies dropouts. Not the 'pasta skirt and broccoli earrings' brigade (as Katy disparagingly calls them) that live here now. Back then, they were the real deal. In this group was a lad called Inch – a dirty blond, scrawny-looking guy. His claim to fame was that his girlfriend Jelly once had a gang bang with three truckers, on a pile of cabbage sacks in the back of their wagon. He was very proud of this story and told anyone who would listen. I thought Inch was marvellous. He had a cool charisma, enhanced by Jelly and his mum, who had an open house to all the 'stoner' kids, and took more drugs than all of them put together. Back then, though, Mandy hadn't yet appeared, so mushrooms and cannabis resin were the drugs of choice in a small village like ours. Our village is still infamous for its excellent magic mushroom spots. I only need to mention where I live to the right people and it's "Ah! Shrooms heaven!" and knowing winks and smiles. Right behind my house is a top spot.

Every dewy morning, just before sunrise from September to late November, you can see shady spectre-like figures in the early morning mist. Of course, they often have a dog because y'know, dog walking and that. The thing is, you can spot a shroomer with a dog decoy a mile off. They keep tripping over the dog as they're busy staring at the ground, and the poo bag is way too light and carefully handled to be full of dog poop. I like the ones who couldn't give a toss and grovel about in the grass with the grim concentration of a nit nurse, picking three and eating four as they go. They're the ones who later probably spend their Sunday lunch at the in-laws, unable to decipher what on earth the roast spuds are talking about, and trying to stop the table, chairs, and lollipop-headed family from disappearing through the floor.

My first and only memory of indulging in a full 'shroom trip' was back in 1978. I was at Inch's mum's house one summer afternoon, probably skiving off school. We were eating Liberty Cap mushrooms wet from the field, out of a waxed bread bag. Inch's mum, Jelly, and another few glassy-eyed kids were smoking resin on a pin from under a beer glass on the scratched and cigarette-burned coffee table. The mushrooms had the texture of glutinous blobs of snot, and I swallowed them until there were none left. Dosage wasn't even heard of. We knew nothing. We were stupid kids rebelling with an equally rebellious adult to assist us. So much of what must have been a horrendous 'trip' has been lost over time, but I remember sitting at the top of Inch's garden steps, facing what looked like a torrent of colour and rushing winding waves of movement down into the busy road below. Some stranger, probably more off their head than I was, helped me down and across the road where I couldn't get into my other friend's front door, because the trilby hat I was wearing wouldn't fit through (I couldn't figure to open the door wider or take the hat off). I currently have a jar of dried magic mushrooms in my kitchen cupboard. They've been there six months or more. I find a mushroom trip is a way more unpredictable experience than LSD, for example, and although I've never had an unpleasant trip, I have had a few occasions where the colours and wonderful effects turned into hours of digging out old negative emotions, which whilst positive in releasing and healing, lingered in the unpleasant creeping anxiety that followed. I learned later that in general 'plant medicines' are best indulged in a natural setting.

I hung about with Inch and his gang for a few weeks and then got back with Rich and went running whenever he called me again. I also had a friend called Julie whom I'd known since primary school. She was a rebellious kid too, but I liked her. We were close mates and hung about together during the holidays. She was the only friend who lived close to me, so when we left school, we both applied for jobs at the local dye mill. The mill was enormous, black, and imposing. It sat in the fog at the valley's bottom and employed a lot of school leavers. Back then we were cheap labour. The area boasted a thriving textiles industry, so we were set on straight away. On our first day, they put Julie on the bottom floor in dyeing, where a lot of the other young school leavers worked, and they put me upstairs in weaving and mending. I truly believe that this event affected my situation with friendships to this day and set in motion a feeling of loneliness and anxiety that has never truly left me.

A local minibus picked up the village employees en route to the mill and took us all to work each day. On my second day, I nervously got on the bus and looked for Julie, as the bus picked her up before me. I spotted her sitting at the back with a loud group of girls from dyeing. They were laughing and shouting at each other, nudging and swearing a lot. As the bus set off, I began to make my way to the back. The girl next to

Julie, who looked at least a couple of years older than us, looked straight at me and shouted,

"Where the f**k do you think you're gonna sit? I'm not shifting!"

Her angry, sneering expression and aggressive manner halted any further movement down the aisle. I was terrified. She stared at me unblinking, daring me to speak or make a move toward her. The other passengers went quiet, waiting to see what drama and entertainment would unfold, and I saw Julie turn away to talk to the girl on her other side. I backed up a few steps and turned around. I stared out of the window the whole journey. Trying not to cry, I waited till they'd gone inside to walk the short pathway to the mill door.

That same day, my manager in weaving sat me with two old ladies in their sixties who had been weavers for years. They were to train me to be a woollen mender. I learned to remove knots and mend loose threads in enormous rolls of cloth that were pulled down from a loom. They set me on removing knots from the scratchy cloth that was used for clothing at the prison in a big town a few miles away. It didn't matter if I missed a few knots, they told me, as it was only criminals wearing the clothes. It was easy, clean work, and I became quite good at it. The ladies told me that the dye department and the weaving department had strange internal politics based on snobbery, and never really had dealings with each other (no kidding!). Every workday was peaceful as I was the 'baby' in a department of (to my sixteen-year-old self) old people. Every morning and evening, however, I stood tensely at the front of the bus by myself and didn't make any eye contact, scared one of the hard girls would spot me and start trouble. Julie never spoke to or acknowledged me again. I was the youngest by at least twenty years in the whole of my department, and while Julie found a group of friends her own age, I was by myself.

Had I had the friendship and support of a peer group, I would have more than likely finished with Rich, as he was already mistreating me. I'd have been socialising and having fun going out with other girls my age. As it was, I had only him and I had only been working for a few months when I found out I was pregnant. Valerie, my manager at work, called me into her office one day and said rumours were going around that I was having a baby. How anyone knew I had no idea, but, in my embarrassment, I hotly denied such a thing and stormed out of her office. I felt all eyes were on me after that and a couple of days later, I nervously asked for a word with her and came clean. Valerie was kind to me and did all she could to make sure I didn't have to lift the heavy rolls of cloth. She also put a stop to any malicious gossip, for which I was very grateful.

I was sixteen years old and terrified. My mum shouted and blamed my dad, and Dad shook his head. Mum snapped at me, "Well, you'd better get rid of it."

I was crying. "I can't, I'm four months along."

She sniffed and told me, "Well, you'd better get married then, because you're not bringing a baby here."

My dad took me to my antenatal appointments, and he even came in and sat with me until they called my name. Looking back, no one knew he was my dad. He could have been my baby's father for all the rest of the waiting room knew. A forty-three-year-old man accompanying a sixteen-year-old heavily pregnant girl invited a few blatant stares. I'm sure they weren't lost on my dad either, but he didn't want me to go in on my own. Mum stayed at home.

I got married at sixteen, with a seven-month bump, at the local registry office. Wearing a pale blue smock dress from C&A, I stood with my parents and Rich's family as the only guests. I had no friends at my wedding because I didn't have any. There was no one there who was anywhere close to my age – just Katy, who at thirteen, was my maid of honour.

My honeymoon night was a stay over at Rich's parents, where they could keep an eye on us (closing the stable door after the horse has bolted springs to mind). I was so immature. I remember being happy because I could now stay up to watch late-night horror films. Rich was already hitting me regularly by this time. Not enough to bruise at first, but enough to make me try harder to be a good wife. Once I was heavily pregnant and ensconced in our tiny council house across the valley, all deals were off. I had no television, no friends, no nothing. Mum and Dad hated Rich and rarely came to see me, so I was beaten regularly and hardly went out, as I was covered in bruises. Rich would go to his parents to eat because we had no money, and sometimes no food. He always found enough cash to get drunk at the pub every night though, while I froze by the coal fire, which often went out due to lack of coal. I would read my meagre collection of paperbacks, dreading the sound of the door when Rich returned. I wasn't allowed to go to his parents with him as they would see my cut lips and swollen face, so I sat alone, just waiting for the key in the lock that meant another smack. One time, Rich got into a fight in a local pub when he was drunk again. Two police officers came to see him, and I was sitting on the sofa with a black eye and cut lip. When he was giving a statement to the policeman in the kitchen, I asked the policewoman who stayed with me to take him to jail because I was so afraid of him. Nothing happened though, and he hit me again once they'd gone because he was angry he would be getting a fine for fighting.

My little girl Melanie was born three weeks overdue, ten days before my seventeenth birthday in 1979, and in many ways, this book is a tribute to her. How unbeknownst to me, her birth, her thoughtfulness, her love and understanding, and that of her husband, Robin, would change the course of my life and introduce me and my husband, Josh, to Mandy. She'd laugh at this. She tells me, "Mum, stop being grateful!"

I'm sure she's secretly pleased, though. I know if I'd changed someone's life for the better, I'd be pleased about it.

With baby-soft brown hair and the smell of sweets, she was my first experience of feeling and receiving genuine love. I knew nothing about babies or how to look after another human, but what I lacked in knowledge, I made up for with kisses. I took her everywhere. It was me and her against the world. Although sometimes things haven't always run smoothly, Melanie has always known how much I love her.

My next-door neighbour, Penny, was a true hippie of the time and was twenty-five. She was tall and softly spoken, with brown curly hair and a constant aura of peace and patchouli. I admired her and wanted to be just like her. She played Bob Marley and The Who records and had a giant poster on her living room wall, advertising Woodstock. Penny had a famous boyfriend, too. He played for a first-division football team and lived in London. He would bring her cannabis and speed, but drugs like speed were still something that happened in films and the big cities – not a little weaving town like ours. I'd never heard of speed and the acid she sometimes took, and I was never offered any. I would sometimes pop round to her house with Melanie, when Rich was in bed, drunk. She was also a single mum, so at least we had something in common.

Penny and I had a cracking communications system going, like morse code but with a northern edge. When she saw Rich going out, past her house, she'd wait a few minutes, then with the iron poker, she'd knock on the back of her fireplace three times. 'Bang'! A quick break, then 'Bang, Bang!' I'd look out on the street and if Rich had disappeared around the corner, I'd message back 'Bang!' Break. 'Bang, Bang!' A moment later she'd appear at my door with her baccy tin with a marijuana leaf on the lid and a couple of cans of Woodpecker cider. We spent many an hour nattering and listening to Fleetwood Mac, until with an hour to go before the pubs shut, she'd go back next door in case Rich caught her in our house. Penny knew what he was like. She could hear it through the paper-thin walls and didn't want to be the cause of any more violence. Originally from a village a few miles away, she still had family there. Unfortunately for me, she got a house exchange to go live close to her mother a year later, so I lost my only friend in the area.

The story of an abusive relationship isn't a pretty one or one I wish to dwell on further in a book of hope and connection; but one day, after a beating that left me with two black eyes and a split lip and with only £1 in my pocket for bus fare, I left my village. I had never travelled over five miles from home, except as a child on holiday. Such was my relationship with my parents that it never once occurred to me to reach out to them for help. It simply wasn't an option. I took Melanie aged one, and we travelled alone to a refuge for battered women I'd read about in the local free newspaper. It was indicative of the times and attitudes that when the bus conductor saw my battered face, he joked chirpily, "You should have ducked, love."

I had called the refuge phone number when Rich was out, and Sandra, one of the ladies who ran the place (we called them the 'workers'), arranged to meet me from the bus, to take Melanie and me there in her car. She was older than me, probably in her late thirties, and had a kind face. Immensely grateful for her being there, I sat silently in the back, hugging Melanie anxiously, watching the strange places flash by. I didn't know where we were or where we were going. By the time we arrived at the refuge, I was shaking. It was an enormous Victorian house which, in its heyday, must have been beautiful and owned by wealthy people in the town. Now it was all crumbling stonework, and the garden was an overgrown jungle of brambles, roof tiles, and broken trees; but it represented safety. Sandra helped carry my small bag of clothes and took me inside.

Immediately, the smell of damp, and greasy cooking hit me as I hesitated in the doorway. Shouting voices and noise came from everywhere and a couple of young mixed-race children dressed only in grubby vests with snot candles on their upper lips ran past us in the hallway.

"Maggi!!!" Sandra yelled up the stairs as she pushed us inside, "Get ya kids some bloody clothes on will ya! How many times do I have to tell you?!"

An equally grubby-looking face appeared from around the bannister grinning.

"Ah fuck off, Sandra! No point wasting grundies when they only piss in 'em! Mucky little bastards."

Laughing good-naturedly, the face disappeared. Wide-eyed with shock at this exchange of viewpoints, I was ushered down the hall, past a horde of women who stared at me with a mixture of curiosity and confrontation. There, I was shown into an empty room where there was a bed with a candlewick bedspread of some generic grey, and a small, scratched, wooden chest of drawers. A single, unadorned lightbulb hung from the nicotine-stained ceiling. Sandra handed me a carrier bag.

"Here are some things to get you by. Tomorrow I'll be back, and we'll get you sorted out."

I barely had time to nod in response before she was gone. I was petrified of all the tough-looking women and didn't dare to go out of my room. As is usually the case with shared adversity, the women were defensive and tough because they were afraid, like me. Some had come from poor backgrounds and had to be tough, but at the time, I had never met people like this before.

I sat on the sagging bed on that first day and tried my best to keep Melanie quiet in case we attracted unwanted attention. We had no money; my last pound having gone on bus fare. I inspected the contents of the carrier bag Sandra had given us – a few tinned ready meals, nappies and milk for Melanie, and a loaf of bread to last until we could go to the Benefits Office the next day. The sounds of shouting and crying children echoed from every room and filled the house. I was so frightened. Going back home wasn't an option as I had no money for a bus and didn't even know the way. I can't remember how long I sat, but it seemed like hours. Cold and hungry, my bladder was bursting, but I was too afraid to go outside my room to the toilet down the hall. Melanie needed something to eat and was squirming in my lap, whining. I jigged her about, hoping I could summon up the courage to peep out of my door and sneak out.

After what seemed like hours, the house eventually fell quiet, and it seemed everyone had either gone out or gone to bed, as it was now dark outside. The dull glow of a streetlamp shone through the grimy window. Suddenly, there was a knock, and the door opened. I stared.

"Hiya!"

It was Maggi, the woman with the bare-bottomed toddlers I'd encountered upon arrival. "You comin' for summat to eat?" She grinned, showing numerous black and missing teeth. "Ya must be fucking starving stuck in 'ere. Who's this then?" She came over and shook the top of Melanie's head affectionately. Melanie, not at all used to such an assault on her person, began yelling at the top of her voice as if someone had poked her with a cattle prod. Without waiting for an answer, Maggi plucked Melanie, now puce in the face and shrieking at the top of her voice, from my arms and headed for the door. That got me moving, and I followed her along the sticky and threadbare carpet, down the narrow hall to the kitchen, nervously looking left and right in case an assailant was hiding in the shadows.

I can still remember that kitchen all these years later. A large, stained, blue Formica-covered table with matching rusty, chrome-legged chairs with ripped seats was next to the window.

"Sit there and I'll get us a cuppa and the kid summat to eat."

Maggi plopped Melanie into a tatty wooden highchair next to the table where she immediately stopped crying, to copy me in watching this loud, but oddly comforting stranger take care of us.

"What's yer name?" she asked, clattering pots and pans without turning around from the battered four-ring cooker.

"Hel…" I croaked in a whisper. I took a breath and tried again. "Helen, and this is Melanie."

I got the words out in a rush and sat in silence again, my stomach feeling clawed out, both with hunger at the aroma of whatever Maggi was stirring, and the awful uncertainty of our situation. She brought over two chipped bowls from a cupboard over the cooker and gave us one each. Pouring some kind of beef stew into mine and giving me a slice of bread, she returned with a warmed pot of baby food for Melanie and a plastic spoon.

"There ya go, nipper." She smiled, and Melanie, easily bought, beamed back, grasped the spoon, and started happily shovelling the food into her mouth and down her front. Maggi turned to me.

"Gerrit eaten," she encouraged. "I don't cook fer every bugger, y'know. I know what it's like to 'ave fuck all."

But I couldn't. I couldn't eat. Maggi quickly swept the bowl out from under me as I slumped, head in my arms, onto the table. She wrapped her arms around me in a hug as I wept. I sobbed and sobbed; the tears seemed endless. A hug felt so alien to me, and I cried until I was exhausted. The kindness of this rough, battered mother who still had the heart to show comfort to others had broken me completely.

Maggi became a friend to me. She introduced me to the other women who I found were all in similar situations and were supportive of us and each other. Maggi and I often went into the local town together, pushing the little ones in their pushchairs. She was funny and very streetwise. Her long hair was always wild, held only in place by errant Kirby grips. Her partner, an enormous Jamaican man, had knocked out her teeth by throwing her on the bed, kneeling on her arms, and punching her over and over in the face while her children watched from their cots. It was his favourite way of making her do as she was told, she explained wryly.

"Got the bastard a right un though," she bragged, grinning. "I left a can of hairspray by the bed on purpose, just knowing it wouldn't be long before I needed it. Anyway, this last time as he chased me into the bedroom, I grabbed the can and sprayed him in both eyes for as long as my finger'd press the trigger, full-on!" She laughed. "While he's chucking himself all over the shop, screaming and rubbing his eyes, I grabbed the lamp by the bed and whacked the fucker with that an' all! Then I grabbed the kids and legged it. I've been in and out of refuges for years, me."

Sadly, a few weeks later, Maggi told me she was going back home. Sandra tried to talk her out of it; the other women tried to talk her out of it. I tried too, but she wouldn't listen.

"He's the kids' dad," she'd say. "He sez he'll get some help and he'll stop drinking. We can buy a house and the kids can have a dog."

He had sold her the dream yet again.

"Appen, we'll see each other back here next time around."

Flashing her toothless grin as she hugged me goodbye, I could see in her eyes she knew she was going back to more abuse. There were only phone boxes with which to contact her and trying to visit her in the situation she was in was out of the question. I never saw Maggi again, but I hope she eventually found the courage to leave for good and got in another few whacks at him before she went.

My parents drove out to visit me in the refuge once in four months and told me that if I didn't come back, they wouldn't be able to come and see me as it was too far. Sandra and one of the other workers explained to them I would return to almost certain danger and that they would support me there and find me a new home away from Rich. But no, I was not to inconvenience my parents. It was twelve miles away; they weren't trailing out there! Katy, however, rode the whole way on her little motor scooter just to see us for an hour. She was my only link to home, and I was so grateful to her for coming. And so, told I had no parental support, I was alone with a toddler at seventeen, in a strange town with no friends. Remember, there were no mobile phones and no internet in the seventies. Alone meant alone back then.

I, too, went back to Rich. I was too young and too afraid to be alone with Melanie. I felt I needed to be somewhere familiar. With Maggi gone, I had nobody again. As she had predicted, she would probably end up back at the refuge, and so did I; but the second time something happened, which meant I would leave my small village and not return until thirty years later.

THE BREAKDOWN

I met my second husband Adrian when he was the DJ at a disco in aid of the refuge. He played *Bat Out of Hell* for me, which impressed me no end as it was over six minutes long (I was easily pleased). Over six feet tall with long brown hair, he wore band t-shirts, was the opposite of Rich in personality, and was only six months younger than me. I was twenty-one by then and Melanie was a sweet-natured four-year-old. Adrian was quiet and initially adoring, lacking in experience with women, with a domineering and emotionally abusive mother. For me, he represented an escape from my past and support in my shaky present. In true 'misery novel' style, two damaged people found each other. He accepted Melanie immediately and loved her dearly. He is her dad, it's that simple. He taught her to read, and ride a bike, and was consistently there for her.

We married in the local registry office, and I wore a borrowed dress with little Melanie as my sole bridesmaid. Again, none of our friends attended, as neither of us had any. Adrian wasn't particularly popular with his peers; he was more of a geek and was interested in music and CB radio. We spent most of our time together listening to records. Again, my pattern of reliance on a man reared its head. We had two other children together, Carl and then Charlotte five years later. Although we were married twenty-one years before divorcing; it was never the love affair we both wanted or the one I yearned for. I needed romantic love and for someone to put me first for a change. I wanted to feel important and be Adrian's priority, but he simply couldn't give me or the children that. He joined a band with one of his cousins and that became his only interest. Throughout our marriage, his sole focus was having his own needs met. This has caused almost all his relationships with family and other partners to increasingly end up fractured or broken. Looking back, I think we both needed stability and never managed to achieve it. Neither of us had the self-esteem to believe we could rise above our poverty-stricken and immature situation, so just lived day to day in chaos.

I had my breasts enlarged in 1983 after a woman came selling cosmetic surgery door-to-door. Can you believe it? She lifted her jumper and showed me her enormous boobs, right there in my living room. I signed up straight away, opting to pay weekly out of money we didn't have. If I had implants to give me bigger and sexier breasts, then surely I'd be more lovable, right? Adrian would then be an adoring and thoughtful husband. Of course, new breasts couldn't fix our problems.

What they did was cement the conviction that if men fancied me, then I was worth loving. My sense of image became all-important to me. I wanted Adrian's band mates to fancy me, the window cleaner, anyone at all. Any man I saw looking at me convinced me further that my self-worth lay in my looks.

I enrolled Melanie in the little church primary school down the road and each day would take her and her brother Carl in his pram for the twenty-minute walk. There I found a friend at last. She was my friend for over thirty years, from the time I met Adrian until four years ago, and her name was Denise. Small, cuddly, and fiercely opinionated, we would chat at the school gates, and we quickly became the most important people in each other's lives. Denise was the friend I had always wanted. She was someone who loved me and put me first, and I did the same for her. We were both in unhappy marriages that were gradually worsening, and I'm sure the adage 'misery loves company' was coined with us in mind. Misery soon became mischief and before long we were inseparable – with secrets. In Denise, I found the love and constant attention I had craved. I have still never laughed with anyone as I laughed with Denise. Every day after school drop-off, we would go to one or the other of our houses and spend the day together smoking, drinking tea, and watching afternoon TV. We were always short of money and often our days were based around thinking up plans of how to make more.

Denise had an old knitting machine, and we came up with this great idea (everything was a GREAT idea) to make kids' tracksuits. I mean seriously, knitted tracksuits; but this was Denise and me and it was the eighties, so anything was possible… or so we thought. Well, we spent days on end, Denise whizzing the machine backwards and forwards, spitting out panels of knitting, and me sewing them together and adding our printed labels (you know, for the 'designer' appeal).

Weeks later, after wrestling and cajoling our crying and embarrassed kids into these knitted horrors, we took photos and made ourselves a catalogue of our wares to hand out to parents at the school gates. What followed was the pinnacle of awfulness. The school was due to hold its annual sports day event, which gave us another great idea – let's get a stall and sell to the posh parents! *Brilliant!* After school, we approached Mr Hall, who was organising the day. He was probably slightly terrified of our enthusiasm, but he agreed we could have a stall and the school would take ten per cent of our profits. Sounded good to us. We were in business!

A few weeks later, the sports day started bright, sunny, and hopeful. Denise and I set off, staggering down the hill to school with Adrian's wallpaper pasting table, a bin liner of tracksuits, and an old biscuit tin to use as a till – recently divested of Garibaldi's over breakfast. What followed was (but only up to that time) the most cripplingly horrendous couple of hours I've ever spent. We lay our stall out beautifully, in a prime position opposite the cake stall, run by the secretary of the Parents Association who, I kid you not, had turned out for the day in the stereotypical cream twinset and pearls. There was no way we could fail. Denise and I sat behind our pasting table, grinning away at every mum who dared to hover six feet away. We were like a pair of starving hyenas surveying the Savannah. Each parent refused to make eye contact or cross the invisible line beyond which they could still sprint and make an escape. Maybe they were scared we might jump on them like a pair of trapdoor spiders, and rugby tackle them to the ground, wrapped in knitted trouser legs.

The morning passed, lunchtime passed, and not one person had so much as glanced at our stuff. We baked and sweated in the sun, while across the way, the cake stall was doing a roaring trade in Victoria sponges and homemade scones. Denise and I watched the kiddie races with our noses in the air. As the day went on and still no one could meet our gazes, we came to the slow realisation that our tracksuits, so carefully made and so proudly displayed, were crap.

Mr Hall sauntered by and smiled kindly, but even as he passed, I reckon he was thinking "Well that's my cut gone west". Clapping ensued as the rosettes and prizes were awarded. With all attention on the kids, we quickly and silently packed up our stall, bought a cake from the cake stall, and sneaked out the back way. And we laughed. We laughed all the way home, dropping bags, and wrestling with the table. We howled with laughter until our eyes streamed and we eventually ran out of breath. The day had been so hilarious, and we were so optimistic and uncrushable that it gave rise the very next day to another great idea.

"Let's write a book of poetry to immortalise these memories!"

Denise eventually left her husband for a mate of her sister's and fled to the furthest reaches she could go – a little village on a tiny island off Orkney. Such was the hold my friendship with her had on me, that I talked Adrian into leaving behind our council house and unemployment to follow them. We packed our stuff, got a house clearance company to pay us a pittance for nigh-on everything we owned, and booked our tickets. How smug we were. We were so sure this was the answer to our problems, that we even took the lightbulbs when we left. We wrapped the house key in a bit of paper with the departing missive: 'Get stuffed!' We posted it through the letterbox of the council offices and drove away, still owing three months' rent arrears. It was, of course, another plan that was never going to solve our problems.

We lived in a rented shed (there is no other accurate description for it) on the same island as Denise. The optimistically called 'village' was on a lump of rock in the middle of the sea. It had five tiny thick-walled croft houses, nine inhabitants, and a lot of scruffy and wild roaming sheep. And it was windy! After a year of living in mud, cold, and even worse poverty on an island boasting only one generator and a fire station that was a bucket on a stick next to the beach, our dreams were shattered. Melanie, age twelve, had to go to the only high school for miles, across the sea in the main town. She had to board there throughout the week and return to the island at weekends. Adrian and I had never considered this, and it broke our hearts. She was so brave, but the stories of how she was bullied there as an outsider wracked us with guilt for a long time after we left.

We had fairy tale ideas of how we would milk cows, grow vegetables, and live a pastoral existence like back in the good old days. All long woollen skirts, rattan baskets, and singing country ditties. Not so. An old lady who lived around the back of Denise's croft house was ninety-six and she had never even seen a fresh peach! When she had to stay in the hospital on the mainland, she was trundled down to the dock in her wheelchair on the forks of a tractor, through the wind and rain. We watched with our hearts in our mouths, howling with laughter and horror in turn, as she lurched and shuddered around, in danger of crashing to the ground, or worse, into the sea, at any moment. Still, we didn't twig what we'd done. The only item that ever filled a local freezer was bread. I found this strange, but Denise explained that bread was the staple diet if no other food could be brought to the island. At times like these, the tiny population survived on toast, eggs, which were dropped liberally all over by the feral chickens, and occasionally someone would go out and shoot a sheep for meat. I feared I had walked unknowingly onto the real-life island of The Wicker Man and became more appalled by the day.

We soon discovered that absolutely every consumable and all other necessities came over from the mainland by boat. "How quaint!" I hear you sigh, except that half the time the boat couldn't sail because of storms and high winds, or the items were out of stock on the mainland. This could go on for months at a time. We would stand on the dock in our shell suits, drenched with sea spray, freezing cold, and thinking wistfully of Pop-tarts and Mars Bars, waiting for a boat that might never come. An hour or so of staring hopelessly out to sea later, we would drag ourselves home, empty-handed and soaked to the skin, for yet another egg-on-toast dinner. When it wasn't freezing and raining, clouds and clouds of tiny black flies would descend on the island. They would get in your hair, eyes, and food. If it wasn't them, it was the Arctic Skua, enormous black and white birds that would have no hesitation in swooping down to attack anyone walking in the open near their nests. Nicknamed 'Bonksies' by the locals, they had sharp beaks and could cause serious injury if they hit you. Most locals on the island had head injuries from them at one time or another. Not that it mattered. The wind was so constant and battering that brushes, combs, and any semblance of a hairstyle were a comedy concept. Everyone looked like a scabby-headed relative of Ken Dodd on the Orkneys.

When we ran out of money and with no permanent employment or housing in sight, we planned our escape. One night, safe in our shed from flies, birds, and gagging from egg-on-toast overload, we called Katy from the only phone box and asked her to book us some tickets on the next available ferry to Aberdeen, which she did without question, bless her. Katy and her husband had a van and agreed to pick us up from the dock a week later to drive us back to Yorkshire. Even now, this amazes me. They drove over four hundred miles just to turn around and take us back. Denise, of course, tried to convince us to stay, but by that point, I'm pretty sure I had trench foot and was determined to seek solace in the modern world again. The morning of our escape dawned fine for once, and we quickly loaded our few possessions onto one of the rare boats in the harbour. With the local postman-cum-fireman-cum-farmer-cum-landlord of our shed yelling that we'd stolen his damp, mouldy, and torn old carpet, we departed for the mainland where our car was parked. Abducting Melanie from the boarding school, we all gave a cheer and headed to the ferry.

We had called the council a week earlier and pleaded insanity, threatening to camp in their offices if they didn't give us our house back. It was a no-brainer for them. They told us we could move back in, and we returned to nothing, and I mean nothing! Arriving back at our council house around midnight the next day, we let ourselves in with a spare key we'd kept when we left (why?).

Click!

Pitch blackness.

Only then did we remember we had taken the lightbulbs with us when we had left. Karma has a timely sense of humour. The next day, I went shopping with our emergency payment from social security. It took all I had not to kneel and kiss the ground outside Tesco. It took us months of scouring the charity shops and lots of help from social services to furnish the house again. Life carried on exactly as before, only without Denise present. With her gone, I was lost. We stayed in touch for a while, but the glaring truth was that Denise had a new life, and I was still stuck.

I was sick and tired of living in poverty. Our phone had been cut off, and we had bills arriving daily. Adrian was qualified as a primary school teacher, but a combination of an inability to accept authority and inherent laziness meant he was on the dole, looking for work. I didn't know how to sort out the mess we were in, and Adrian figured the best way was to ignore it and play computer games. In a moment of madness and utter genius, I had a lightbulb moment, which proved to set me on another path entirely. I applied to go to university.

As a mature student, I would qualify for a grant. What other way was there to get a fast lump sum of money to get us out of the mess we were in? I mail-ordered a university prospectus, and when it arrived, I pored over the different degree courses I could apply for. The more I read, the more I believed I could do it. What if I got a degree and a good job? Suddenly the grant was taking a back seat. I wanted to do something with my life and for the kids to have everything they deserved. After attending a couple of open days at the university, I signed up for a degree course in English Literature and Language. I loved English at school and am still an avid reader. It would take four years to finish, but as it was part-time, so I could work while I studied. The tutors were enthusiastic about the course, stressing that every job required excellent language skills so we would be certain to be snapped up by an employer.

University gave me confidence, but it was hard work juggling the children, a part-time job as a waitress, and studies. Adrian made it even harder for me because it took my focus off him. In retrospect, he was right, it did. At Uni I was Helen. Not someone's mum, not someone's wife – just Helen, and I felt free to be myself. I enjoyed the work and felt validated every time a tutor gave me a good mark or a positive comment. At

Uni, I had people who believed I was good enough and told me so.

The next four years seemed to fly by because I was engaged and busy all the time. I had Uni friends and we often studied and went out for lunches together. Each class was an escape from the worries of home and my depressing relationship with Adrian. Then, suddenly, my studies were at an end. I went into the university building for the last time to hand in my final dissertation, walking along corridors where I had paced nervously on my first day there. I walked past the classrooms where I had once sat, puzzling over countless essays. For a final time, I went down the stairs, past the vast lecture theatres where I had listened with awe to doctors of English explaining political writing. Reaching the small admin office, I paused for a second before posting my dissertation through the secure letterbox. Opening the door to the street a few minutes later, the feeling of loss was like a punch to the throat as realisation hit me. I had nowhere to go, I had no classes to be at, no deadlines to work to, and even worse, no colleagues to spend time with. I was no longer free to wander the halls and be Helen. I felt institutionalised and abandoned. A few months later, I was awarded a B. A. (Hons) 2.1 degree and was back where I had started four years previously.

This time I refused to be defeated, and buoyed by enthusiasm and confidence in my educational value, I began to apply for jobs. The choices proved to be extremely limited. It didn't take long to realise that my degree was worthless unless used in conjunction with another that qualified me for a specific role. It impressed employers, but in addition, they wanted either experience or a backup qualification. After a few knock-backs, I managed to get a job as a teaching assistant at my son, Carl's, high school on a twelve-month contract. I should have known it wouldn't work out, even before I started. All of Carl's friends, who regularly came calling for him at home, attended the school and were in many of the classes with me. They were good kids, but as befitting of their ages, they tormented both Carl and me mercilessly. They would act up in class, hoping to get a rise out of me. The teachers weren't at all happy about having to deal with the disruption, either. On one occasion I was heading back to the staff room, when one of Carl's friends, a tall lad, taller than me, ran up behind me, picked me up, and spun me around before plonking me back on my feet and running off laughing. Of course, I reported the lad (I had little choice), but it became evident that I had neither the confidence nor the aptitude to be a disciplinarian, and the kids would always take advantage of me being Carl's mum.

When the twelve months were up, my contract was not renewed, and I wasn't upset about it. What followed was a depressing variety of roles taken purely to keep the wolf from the door. I had imposter syndrome and didn't dare apply for jobs that invited degree-level applicants, because I had no experience in a large and competitive work environment. Although Adrian had previously been down the university route, he wasn't encouraging. I couldn't drive in those days, so when I did finally get a job as a library assistant three miles away, he refused to give me lifts there. If there was no money for public transport a week before his payday, I walked there in all weathers, while he sat watching television at home. The ultimate insult was when he found me a job at the local taxi rank. The hours were from six at night until two in the morning and the wage was £1 an hour, which even then was a pittance. I can't believe I stuck that job out for almost eight months.

THE END OF THE LINE

What followed was almost inevitable. I feel nothing but shame about it, and almost entirely for my children Melanie, Carl, and little Charlotte, who was around four when the roller coaster of rot and damage set in. How I wish that I had had the fortitude and self-esteem I have now. I would have walked away, head high, and made a life for us. Looking again for love and attention, I became way too close to a guy who was in Adrian's band. Adrian was more than happy to palm me off on him, by slipping him a fiver to take me to the local pub music quiz. It meant he could stay at home in front of the telly and not have to make any effort. The chap in question was more than happy to step into the breach. Our kids suffered from my selfish desire to get away and change my life. Anyone who tells me that affairs are 'playing away' has never seen the fallout as I have. There is no 'play'. Affairs destroy everyone in their path; like a runaway truck, they crush anyone who gets in their way. I sneaked about and wallowed in the misery that followed when the affair inevitably ended, and I feel nothing but shame at stealing a year of my children's lives. Melanie looked after me as though I were a child –

something a young teenage girl should never have to do. I will have those regrets always, as I feel my actions had a profound impression on her. At eighteen, she entered the world of photographic modelling, and I know it wasn't always the career she had hoped it would be. There were times I should have been Mum, instead of trying to be her 'mate'. I supported her without warning her of the potential pitfalls, and some might say I lived vicariously through her, which later proved to damage our relationship. It is testimony to her and her alone that she's the well-balanced, funny, and successful woman she is today.

One Valentine's Day was yet another occasion when Adrian punished some perceived slight. I received nothing at all from him. Denise, however, sent an enormous bouquet of roses, a card, and chocolates for me. Adrian was livid, but he would never cross Denise. He knew I would have chosen her by that point. She knew all my secrets, hopes, and dreams, and made sure she fulfilled them all. She was a devoted friend, but sadly, our friendship was based on control.

When the affair ended, I realised I couldn't keep trying to find love elsewhere and hurting my kids in the process. Adrian didn't even attempt to change. Although I told him about the affair in a last-ditch attempt to open his eyes to our problems, he refused to listen. Finally, I did the right thing and left. Looking back, I can see that by the time I had begun the affair, Adrian and I were already over.

After ten years, Denise moved back from Orkney to a few miles away from me, and we tried to pick up where we left off. It was Denise who rallied to the cause when, in 2004, I finally plucked up the courage to find myself a flat. I left Adrian on one of the nights when he was watching football at his brother's house. Such was sympathy for my situation that a couple of his friends at the time kept my secret and helped me to move. I reckon both secretly imagined I'd be *very* grateful, but not this time! Adrian begged, promised, and threatened, but I refused to go back. I had somewhere to live, and fourteen-year-old Charlotte had decided to come with me. I had taken nothing from our home other than the washing machine, my computer, and my personal possessions, but I was hopeful about our new start.

Adrian called at the flat not long after I left and demanded to be let in because he said he wanted to know what conditions Charlotte would be living in. Looking scathingly around at my bare flat, he sneered, "You'll be here for the rest of your life."

Ironically, just over a year later, I was arranging a mortgage on a little Victorian cottage just outside the area, but a lot was to happen before that.

A few days after I'd moved into the flat, Denise came to visit.

"I've got you a housewarming present," she said, grinning with mischief.

Considering she was empty-handed, I figured in all likelihood it wasn't the toaster I'd hoped for. Adrian's friend had set up my computer and internet connection, which in those days meant dial-up. Sitting down on the sofa, Denise asked me to log on, which I did. I was a bit annoyed as I just wanted to tell her all my news and show her around the flat.

"Right," I told her, matter-of-factly, "I'm off to put the kettle on."

I left her to it and went into the kitchen to make us both a cuppa. Upon my return five minutes later, row after row of eligible, weird-looking, and desperate men had appeared on the screen! Denise proudly informed me she'd signed me up for gold membership on a dating site called 'Date the UK'. *Oh great!* I felt cross and not at all grateful. *Here we go again*, I thought. Men and trouble went hand in hand, and I'd just escaped both. I explained to her in no uncertain terms that I wasn't in the least bit interested and told her to turn the computer off. Denise was never one to be told anything though and carried on perusing the virtues of the singletons on the screen. Bristling with irritation, I leaned over her shoulder, intending to press the 'off' key myself, but stopped in my tracks when I spotted a cute guy with long, wavy hair. Long hair has always been my Achilles heel when it comes to men – I love it.

"Him there." I pointed. "Write, 'You are Gorgeous', then come and get your coffee, will you?"

Denise did as I had instructed. Minutes later, we were talking and laughing, ten to the dozen, as we always did; the dating site forgotten.

Of course, the universe had a good giggle at my expense when a few days later, there pinged a message into my inbox from Mr Gorgeous. It said he'd seen my message after logging onto the site to delete his membership. He asked if I'd like to chat. I mean, he *was* gorgeous, and I was alone, so what was wrong with chatting, right? The trouble wasn't that he had a car, loved festivals, lived over a hundred miles away, *and* was willing to travel to meet. All that was just perfect… the trouble was that he was also twenty-five. Another trouble was that when Denise had signed me up to the site, she had changed my age to make me two years younger.

"Because you know, any woman over forty is not going to 'give out', is she?" Denise cheekily informed me, demonstrating with a pelvis-thrusting, arm-pumping motion.

Poor Josh. I felt desperately sorry because he told me he'd already had a relationship based on deception with an older woman. I also was upset because I liked this guy a lot. He seemed kind and decent, which were alien qualities to me when it came to men.

Fortunately, after a long and angst-ridden phone call, Josh realised that I wasn't out to trap him, and so we began to see each other in person. Once a month at first, then twice, then every week, as we fell in love. Of course, I got the typical warnings:

"He's young; it'll only last six months. You have kids, and he won't want them," from Katy, and, "Have a bit of fun, then dump him and get someone more grown-up," from Denise.

Even now, I know the sensible thing would have been to have listened because Josh and I have had some predictable issues around maturity in our relationship. In retrospect, I wasn't ready to trust another man. I could have ended up as the cover story of Take-a-Break magazine because I was still so naïve.

Fortunately, our families accepted our relationship. My children liked Josh and grew to love him, and currently, we are about to celebrate our eighteenth wedding anniversary. Josh has endless patience and is one of the gentlest and most thoughtful men I have ever met. He puts every family member above himself, and he succeeded in renewing my faith in marriage. It's strange to think that he and I were never meant to meet. He had given up, I had given up, and yet here we are now, travelling the Mandy pathway, after all these years together. I will forever be grateful to Denise for signing me up to the dating site that day, but the age-on-my-profile issue wasn't the last time Josh experienced Denise at her controlling best.

In stark contrast to me now, my ex-husband, Adrian, is still single and cripplingly socially awkward. Being completely self-absorbed, he's unhappy as a result. We are still casual friends and see each other at family gatherings. He gets on well with Josh, and all I wish for him is that he could accept the lessons I've had to learn and open his heart to others. I guess that's his journey, if or whenever he is ready. It's a sad fact that you can't help everyone, no matter how hard a time they seem to be having. Help and being open to help are a matter of personal timing. If you aren't yet receptive enough to accept your shortcomings, then the lessons are wasted.

I had so much to learn and was still so set in my ways. When my divorce came through from Adrian, I spent a lump sum on solving my current problems as I saw them. I booked a cosmetic surgery package in Prague. I presumed a face-lift would keep me looking young, beautiful, and irresistible to Josh. I was just forty-one at the time. Of course, Josh said I didn't need it and I ignored him. He was twenty-six; what did he know? And anyway, at that time I didn't even know if he might stick around for very long. In the end, I had a face-lift, neck-lift, and eye-lift and I nearly bled to death in the process. Josh told me later that during the surgery, an artery in my neck had been cut accidentally and a specialist surgeon had to be flown in to stop my bleeding. The clinic had fobbed off his calls and denied him access to see me, which, of course, terrified him. When they finally allowed him in to visit me, I was semi-conscious, with a long bolster pillow under me. It was completely drenched in blood, almost to my feet. Unbeknownst to me, thousands of miles away, my sister Katy sobbed with worry. None of this put me off doing it again, though. I later had my eyelids and under eyes surgically enhanced, but this time in England. Nowadays, I still occasionally catch myself equating my physical attractiveness to my self-worth. I recently decided not to have any more surgery – but would you believe that it was a recreational drug that helped to change my perspective?

Melanie's second husband was called Robin, and she was finally happy. Robin was a talented musician, good-looking, and as disorganised as Melanie was organised. His whole outlook was and still is, accompanied by a cheeky grin and oodles of charm. We all love him dearly. He and Melanie are cut from the same working-class cloth, woven tightly to make satin. I have never had any doubt that they were meant to be. As cheesy as it sounds, their wedding truly was like a fairy tale. They planned it all themselves, over many months. The result was very 'them', and it was wonderful – a 'reet' Yorkshire wedding, flat caps and all. There was a bird of prey display, a live band, Yorkshire tea, and dancing. Melanie was a picture of joy. My heart leapt with pride at her beauty, as she walked down the aisle with Robin in his tweed cap, Kelly, and Louis, their tiny son holding Melanie's train.

My children were all settled and happy. Charlotte was studying to be a beauty therapist, and it was the ideal job for her. She was of slim build, with high cheekbones and catlike eyes, and blessed with the most gorgeous, nearly black, long hair. Back when she was a teen, it had given her a striking, almost Gothic look. Now settled with her boyfriend Adz, they had two little boys, Ethan and Peter.

Both of my daughters are stunningly attractive. They benefited from the perfect combination possible of less-than-perfect parental genes. For example, I have a bump on my nose, but the combination of genes smoothed itself out nicely so that Charlotte got her dad's straight one. Melanie berates me for her chubby knees, but I reckon they look slim and lithe on her – she has an amazing figure. Nothing wrong with our knees; they get us around, anyway. Both Melanie, Charlotte, and I share a sense of humour that embraces what we call 'eye-faces' and observation at its keenest. We howl with laughter at the most unlikely (and often unacceptable) things. We're all very different, yet alike in so many ways.

My blue-eyed, blond, smiley son, Carl, was with his girlfriend, Jemma, and their three girls, Gilli, Edie, and Jasmine. I was so proud of Carl's achievements, as he hadn't had it easy, either. He had separated from a previous girlfriend, but her teenage son and Carl had grown very close. When they split, he continued to see the lad and still does. I admire Carl's loyalty, kindness, and sense of fun. He'd give anything he had to anyone.

Yes, all my children were secure and happy. Everything was rosy… so why did I still not feel whole?

Every few weeks over the thirty years I was away from my village, I had thought of it. For over eighteen years, Josh and I had been employed by a global telecommunications company. We worked in the same building as one another but in different offices, so were in secure employment. Our little cottage, however, had started to leak from the basement kitchen, upward, and from the roof downward, so we were considering putting it up for sale. It was a money pit we would never manage to fix. Some of our early marital issues were also based around the time we lived there, and I wanted to leave. More than that, I wanted to go home, back to the village I grew up in.

I still sought love and approval, and I still had an on/off relationship with my parents, and I unwittingly projected all my insecurities onto Melanie. Before meeting Robin, she had survived a troubled and abusive marriage, and I supported her, but I could have been a better granny to my granddaughter, Kelly. I loved her and had been present at her birth, but I was without the responsibility of young children for the first time since being sixteen, so mentally I blanked out playing that role again. Of course, no parents, not even mine, do what they do to intentionally damage, and neither did I. I simply didn't pause to think.

Had I been introduced to Mandy sooner, I'm certain a lot of my past regrets wouldn't have happened. I can appreciate that for someone I'm telling this story to, it's hard to believe, but it's easy for me to say with conviction that Mandy may well have changed my attitude and altered my views significantly.

My kids still had their issues, as we all do. I would try to help as much as I could, but again, my past came back to pick away at them. I wasn't stable enough to let them make their own mistakes and simply be supportive. In trying to help, I often made them feel like lesser people by taking over and playing one off against the other. Melanie was always kind and supportive, a fellow Pisces to a 'T'. Later, though, she and Charlotte could no longer cope with my narcissistic personality and the effect it had on them. I could sometimes be smug, controlling, and judgmental. Eventually, the crows came home to roost, and I found myself cut out of their lives and unwelcome in their homes. By this time, Josh and I had bought a lovely house just on the outskirts of the village where I was born, and I should have been happier than I'd been in years. However, I spent my days crying and my nights sleepless and plagued with misery and regret.

Carl, too, was barely speaking to me, and I fell into an almost suicidal depression. The thought of living without my children was unimaginable. I was not my mum, I couldn't do it, and if I had to listen, then I would – not only listen but be heard too. Melanie and Charlotte told me that I lay all my insecurities firmly on their shoulders. I still thought I had to be beautiful to be loved; I was constantly seeking to be gorgeous and having a younger husband didn't help my insecurities. My kids were in my slipstream. I was jealous of their youth and possibilities because mine had never lived, nor shone. I had made them feel as my mum had made me feel – not good enough. Yet I loved them. I loved them without reservation or condition, so how had it come to this? Mostly, I was jealous of their easy friendships, their connections, and how others loved and trusted them. Why couldn't I have those things too?

It took a few years for the change to happen, to the extent that Josh and I considered moving to the street next to Denise and her new husband, Alan. We put in an offer on a house there. Fortunately, I saw the pattern of dependence emerging again and Josh could see the issues we would have if we lived so close to Denise, and we changed our minds. Thank goodness we did. Denise dropped me like a hot brick once she saw the control had finally dissipated. I was stronger with Josh. The realisation that my friendship with Denise had always been set into a grounding of mutual misery and disrespect signed the death knell.

Josh and I bought the three-bedroomed semi with sizable gardens in my old hometown. It's indicative of the decline of Denise's and my friendship that I chose not to tell her when we put an offer in for this house, as I didn't trust her not to attempt to somehow sabotage it.

This was a time of great emotional strain on Josh and me, as his mum also died that year. She had been ill for a long time with various issues, but after many exploratory surgeries, they diagnosed her with cancer of the bowel. What followed were long journeys down south, each time afraid to come home in case she took a turn for the worse. When not visiting her, we made constant phone calls to support Josh's dad. For the last few weeks of her life, she was moved to a hospice. After a late-night call from Josh's sister, we drove as fast as was safe to be with her. Tragically for Josh, we arrived too late. His dear mum had died less than fifteen minutes before we got there. Grieving Josh then had to contend with his dad suddenly turning up at ours with a new girlfriend. We both tried to welcome her, as we understood that taking care of his mum had been draining on Josh's dad for many years. However, in finding someone new, he almost completely blanked out his family. Josh and his sisters were abandoned whilst still grieving. It was awful to see Josh's pain, especially as he tried hard to hide it.

I could see him falling into a similar depression to mine, and it was a struggle to help each other. One night, after months of him not eating properly and just sitting in silence, I encouraged him to talk to me about his sadness. It was worse than I had thought. Josh was struggling every single day. He had been allowed a few days off work to attend his mum's funeral, but was under tremendous pressure to get back to work straight after and to take on more responsibility. Always one to step up and help, he had been loaded with work because the company knew he wouldn't say no. Alongside his grief, his desire to support me, and his reluctance to let his boss down had broken him. I managed to convince him to make an appointment to see the doctor. Each carrying emotional burdens, we were drifting apart. I felt powerless to help Josh, and he was either in tears or a numb silence that terrified me – especially when he occasionally cried that he no longer wanted to live as he was a burden to me. He felt he should be helping me in grieving for the kids. Josh believed that if he wasn't around, I would have the house paid for by his employers and that I would find someone who could give me the life I wanted. Life had become a constant dragging of ourselves through suffocating sadness.

I do know that nobody, unless they are a psychopath, has the intention to hurt others, and neither did I. I couldn't see the harm I was doing to my relationships with Melanie, Charlotte, and Carl and in retrospect, of course, I should have. However, I was willing to do anything to learn the solution, and it was a hard lesson to learn. Never have I felt more distraught than when I couldn't reach my children. I couldn't hold them, laugh with them, tell them I loved them, nothing. I too eventually turned inward and rejected all comfort from Josh or my sister Katy.

Denise, who was still on the scene, was basking in my misery and how she could be involved in it. I had found myself in my pain, allowing her to disrespect my children and call them names. I thought she was being supportive. I didn't see it at the time, but when Josh warned that her influence was destructive, I thought again. I was putting her and my own needs first, not theirs. They had been right all along. My poisonous lack of esteem had made me tolerate so much disrespect, projecting it like a virus onto my children. I knew I had to change. Facing my mistakes and my fears was hard – the hardest thing I've ever done. I booked myself in to see a counsellor, and I talked about my parents, my husbands, my children, and my life.

I went to see Melanie, and she allowed me in. I held Louis in my arms and dripped hot tears onto his soft baby head whilst my first love, my beautiful Melanie, just stood and watched me sob with not a touch of pity on her face. I didn't recognise the cold, hard person I was seeing. This wasn't my daughter. This wasn't the thoughtful and caring Melanie that knew me so well that she bought me a beautiful, sexy, and classy outfit when I had my hysterectomy, knowing I'd feel less feminine. Melanie had a heart so big it could envelop the world given the chance, and I had made her like this.

It was slow progress. There were times I shouted at them about all the unfairness of *my* life, how I couldn't navigate the mountains of misery, nor crawl up through the layers of confusion that had got me to this point of being ostracised. I begged and blamed and promised. And then, weak from the effort, I emerged anew. I was Helen. I was also Mum and Granny, and I loved all three personas. All three loved each other, and we all had one goal: to connect with the ones we adored and not be defined by the past.

I spoke to Denise less and less about my personal issues, and I began to realise that a friend who can't be happy for you quickly becomes an enemy. She visited us in our new house once, but that was the last time I saw her. We haven't been in touch for a few years now and I have no urge to rekindle the connection. Sadly, it gave me an unrealistic view of what friendship is, and I'm still learning to understand that a person doesn't have to be enmeshed in my life to be a good friend.

MUM, MEET MANDY

I adore my little grandson Louis and was more than happy to have him sleep over now and again. Babysitting, or 'bonding', as Melanie liked to call it, to seal our fate, was now a joy to me. Whenever Melanie and Robin had a party for friends and family, we would... hang on... friends and...

"Oh, are Carl and Jemma coming?"

"Yeah, depends on if they can get a sitter. We asked them, anyway."

"Ah," I said, "but if we're babysitting, we won't be able to come, will we?"

There was a short but very definite pause before she said, "It's kinda not that type of party, Mum."

A slightly longer pause from me followed whilst I digested her reply. Drugs and alcohol. It had to be. To be less immediately judgmental, which I admit, is one of my worst traits, I responded with, "Okay, what kind of party is it? Tell me – I'm interested."

There followed one of the most bizarre conversations between mum and daughter you're ever likely to hear. Melanie talked about what a 'recreational' drug is, what they feel like, and how they connect people. Melanie informed me that the one they used made a party special. She assured me it was completely different from 'hard' drugs like heroin, which can send the user down the black hole of addiction and self-destruction. It was all very thought-provoking stuff, which I was still thinking about later and long into the night.

I considered how Josh was such a closed book, his breakdown, and how he would benefit from being more open with others instead of feeling he had no one to talk to. Although Josh was taking antidepressants and having counselling, his emotions were on a constant tightrope. Our intimacy had flagged as he slept most of the time when he wasn't at work. I would lie awake, unable to rest from worrying about where our marriage was going. I thought of how I desperately needed the same kind of comfort he craved. I wanted my lovely, happy-go-lucky Josh back. I thought an awful lot, unable to shake the feeling that trying 'something' could well be the answer.

The next time I spoke to Melanie, I summoned up the courage to ask her if we might be able to try a bit of a recreational drug. I was afraid to tell Melanie too much about why, as I didn't want to give her something else to worry about, or to be too demanding of her attention while we were rebuilding our relationship.

What followed turned out to be a quite justified reel of instructions from Melanie, and a "yes."

"You can have a bit each in a capsule, but if you decided not to go ahead, please don't throw it away. We'll take it back, as it's not cheap."

A few days later, the capsules containing some beige-coloured powder, apparently called 'Mandy', were in situ on top of the key cabinet on my kitchen windowsill – and there they stayed. Josh and I peered at them together, wandered off, and discussed when we'd take the plunge. We'd wait a day or two, pick them up, shake them, and peer again.

The two capsules sat there for over a month like the proverbial elephant in the room, with both of us giving them side glances every time we were in the kitchen making tea. A pair of right cowards, we were. We were just too afraid of the unknown, and with no one to guide us or to be there if anything went wrong, nerves got the better of us. It wasn't going to happen, and I was too embarrassed to tell Melanie we had changed our minds, so we chucked them in the bin. Melanie hadn't forgotten, of course, so we had to come clean in the end. We confessed we were too scared to take them, but had been too sheepish to tell her. I don't recall her response, but it was probably peppered with expletives and disappointment. It wasn't until a year later that she and Robin trusted us to meet Mandy again officially.

We would occasionally drop in at their house for a cuppa on our way back from shopping on a Saturday morning. On a couple of occasions, there would be a pair of what we could only describe at the time as 'scummy deadbeats' slumped on the sofa. This pair of glassy-eyed, dishevelled scrotes went by the names 'Van Gav' and 'Lee'. I willed Melanie and Robin not to leave us with this shifty-looking pair while they made tea, although they seemed more than happy to do so. Although we both felt distinctly uncomfortable, there was no way I was going anywhere. There was no doubt in my mind that as soon as we left them alone, they would be stealing my daughter's possessions and probably be pissing on the carpet to add insult to injury.

Josh and I perched on the edge of the sofa, protecting Melanie's home, like the smug, disapproving parents we were. We just knew this shifty couple had been smoking weed or something equally dodgy and were not impressed. So, there we were, a more mismatched quartet than you've ever seen – the layabouts not making eye contact, and parents bristling with discomfort. All the while, Melanie and Robin laughed and chattered away in the kitchen. Knowing them, the laughter was probably at the horror of the situation for us lot only yards away in the living room. I was so happy that my grandchildren were sleeping over at their other grandparents' house, so they wouldn't have to witness this social sewerage so close to their toy box.

Josh and I made our excuses and left after half an hour or so, whispering to one another that we wouldn't drop in without an invitation in future. And so, we waited…

Melanie and Robin had invited us over after tea one Saturday evening. The very first COVID lockdown had been announced for the following week and it was a while since we'd seen them, so we were happy to accept. It was quite unusual for them to be free, as they were often out or had friends over. The kids were staying with their other grandparents for the weekend, so we had the house to ourselves, meaning we could chat openly. You know how it is when the floodgates open – suddenly I was spilling out months of loneliness, anxiety, and depression. Josh just listened, barely contributing at all. Melanie and Robin already knew some details of his breakdown, but not all. They just sat and listened, not interrupting or offering advice, just patiently letting us get it out. At some lull in the conversation, probably from our need to draw breath and because they were bored to death of my whining, Robin and Melanie disappeared into the kitchen for drinks. A moment later, Robin reappeared with a couple of glasses.

"Here," he offered with a grin. "Let's have a magic drink."

Josh looked up.

"What harm can it do?" he said, dully. "We might all be dead this time next year."

I rolled my eyes in despair and the merest flicker of eye contact occurred between us. As I turned away for a second, Josh drank the contents of his glass down in one. I couldn't believe he'd done it, so in a 'sod it' and fear-of-missing-out moment, I did the same.

We *knew,* even without saying anything, that the 'magic' was something more than alcohol. We *knew* we were crossing an invisible and undiscussed line. We also knew that the line once crossed would shatter our brittle steps to the moral high ground forever. Despite that, we both drained our glasses with only the merest hint of hesitation. I have heard a million times since that another drug, called DMT, will find you once you're ready to receive its gifts. MDMA was the same. That night, Melanie, Robin, *and* Mandy knew we were ready.

We have lost much of that first experience in the slight fog of memory that sometimes accompanies MDMA usage – especially the first one. I know we arrived at around eight at night and had gone home much, much later in the morning. I also remembered that I had danced. I had told Melanie and Robin of my crushing loneliness, of how I felt I fitted nowhere, and my need to connect with people like me. As I talked, I kept on dancing. I know now that my 'dancing' involves hours of moving my arms and legs around in the manner of the Hydra's snakes – no rhythm, not even any music half the time – just slow, mellow movement. It hadn't even been a decision, more of a compulsion.

Josh was sitting down in a big armchair, relaxed and smiling. He doesn't mind admitting that he has always been rather reticent to share his feelings. He shared them with me, but even then, I knew he still held a lot back. He seems to always be analysing a conversation as to how much he can reveal. This time, he opened up. Josh told us all as a group the effect his breakdown had. Some I knew, a lot I didn't. He talked of his mother's death, his hopes, and his dreams. As Josh talked, he began to remove his trousers! There I was, dancing away to my inner disco and there was Josh – in my daughter and son-in-law's living room, pant-less and chatting away like it was nothing out of the ordinary. I kept glancing over in case I had to intercept a stray knacker. Thank goodness he had kept his boxer shorts on.

As I swayed and moved, I talked some more. Dancing away, up in the clouds somewhere, I was still more than capable of shock.

"Er, babe, your trousers! What are you doing?"

Melanie and Robin, evidently unfazed by this sudden and uncharacteristic disrobing, didn't mind at all.

"Mum, he's fine, don't embarrass him," muttered Melanie, motioning me to shut up without breaking eye contact with Josh. She continued to smile and nod at him as he carried on talking.

Okay. Right. Well, that's alright then, I reckoned, and just went with the flow. I could feel the MDMA rising in my body, what I now know as the 'coming up' feeling. I was with it, riding the wave with absolute euphoria. Up, up, up… until the peak hit. Drawing in deep lungfuls of air, I felt I could fly on the high of emotion and joy I felt. I gazed around at these three people I loved so much, and with whom I felt such a pure connection – such a oneness of spirit… then the calm enveloped me again. Of course, they call this feeling 'rolling', which is a perfect description. It's a roller-coaster – rising, then rushing down, rolling on the waves in the ocean like a surfer. It's rolling down a grassy hill, laughing and breathless.

Hours passed in what seemed moments, and we talked and shared our lives in a way like never before. Josh and I hugged each other and kissed – not sexually, just feeling the pure love and closeness, smiling and releasing the anxiety. Much later, and back home in our bed, we made love with an intimacy that had sadly become just a memory. Josh described to me the feel of my skin, and the smell of my hair, and told me sincerely how beautiful he thought I was. Our lovemaking that night was a sensory celebration of who we were. We held each other in an embrace so close that I could see myself and my life in his eyes. Even now I believe that the phrase 'life-changing moment' is overused. A life-changing moment is a rare occurrence, but this was certainly one of them. Mandy showed us not only how to deal with our lives, but also changed the way we lived from then on.

Of course, Josh and I talked about the experience the next morning. We talked about it for hours. What had shifted in us so that neither of us would refuse what we had been offered? We didn't know then that it was MDMA (Methylenedioxymethamphetamine) in the drink. We just knew it was *something*. What Robin had given us was a scraping of rock (or crystal), which is the way MDMA looks until it's been made into the ecstasy pills I now prefer, solely because MDMA tastes disgusting. It's also stronger than most pills, which can contain a mixture of caffeine, chalk, and other substances.

Josh was having difficulty processing his experience. He said that the feelings had manifested themselves as a compulsion to release himself, both physically and verbally, which is why he had felt the urge to remove some of his clothing. He felt restricted, and Mandy wanted to let him out! It was also quite a revelation when he haltingly admitted that the release was also literal in the way it can only be for a man, but without the erection or sexual feelings that usually accompany an ejaculation. He said he didn't even notice until he got dressed. I wasn't all that surprised, if I'm honest, because it made perfect sense to me. My lovely, kind, understanding, patient-to-a-fault Josh had succumbed to Mandy telling his body that it was finally okay to let go, without mockery or judgment.

We spent a lot of time talking about the experience and an equal amount of quiet contemplation, trying to process our feelings.

Melanie called later the following day, and, in a slightly high-pitched voice, doubtless caused by the anxiety of what she and Robin had done, she asked how we were. I could almost feel her sagging with relief when, "Fantastic!!!! Best night EVER!!" was the dual hollering from our end of the phone. She told me later that she sprung awake the morning after, wide-eyed and mortified as to what had happened, and had fretted about whether we would be ashamed or angry. We were neither – in fact, we were the absolute opposite. We believed we'd found the answers to questions we hadn't even thought of yet.

Characteristically for me, I was afraid. I felt more scared than I had been *before* Melanie and Robin introduced us to Mandy. We had been gifted with a conduit to healing and releasing both Josh and me, but what if it never appeared again? *Come back, Mandy! Don't leave us after giving us a glimpse into what could be!*

I was confused, as well as scared. Surely MDMA, Mandy, Molly, or ecstasy (it seemed to have different names in different places), was a recreational drug for ravers and parties in Ibiza? I'd seen films about it, and they hadn't portrayed it like our experience at all. We met Mandy in a living room in a small northern town – my daughter's living room at that. Where were the strobe lights, thumping music, and jumping, sweaty bodies when *I* felt the medicine?

I felt it had cured me of some awful affliction. I bet I drove Melanie bonkers with texts, questions, and enthusiastic ramblings. Each one she patiently answered, and she humoured me until I eventually ran out of steam. Nevertheless, I was still lonely. Nothing had changed except that I knew I *could* connect. I wanted to change and meet people like me. I have never felt such an urgency to begin a journey in my life!

Journey. Path. Words that are so overused and cliché that almost every person on social media is on one. We all live our lives like Dorothy and Toto meeting the Tin Man, Scarecrow, and the Cowardly Lion, linking arms and skipping along together in search of the magic that will heal us and take us home. How many times had I read on Facebook 'Your Vibe Attracts Your Tribe'? It doesn't at all. W*hat a load of rubbish*. If that was the case, where was my tribe? I wanted one more than anyone. Despite that, they hadn't appeared. The simple fact is that my vibe had been repelling my tribe and keeping them at arm's length. My judgmental, acidic, and snarky vibe had not been on my side for years.

Waking up one morning, I began to think about my work situation, where I spent eight hours a day with the same people. Eighteen years ago, not long after Josh and I met in 2004, we got jobs for the telecommunications company that grew to be the global market leader. This was the job for which I'd spent four years of study to get. I had proudly shown the interviewer my degree certificate, only to realise I would be in training with people of all ages from a variety of backgrounds, from a sandwich shop assistant to an astrophysics graduate. My degree and accompanying £8000 student debt meant nothing here. What mattered was that I was a great communicator. We both started at the bottom and worked our way up. For the whole of those eighteen years, I made not one close friend. I had close colleagues, of course, ones I got on better with than others. We'd pass our working week laughing and helping each other on cases.

I started in sales, as did most of the new people, selling contracts and conducting credit checks on new customers. I logged on one morning and my first call of the day was from a guy who was annoyed that we had to conduct a check on him.

"Hello, Helen speaking. How can I help?"

"Hiya, I'm just calling because I don't see why I have to have a credit check just to get a mobile phone."

This was a common query. Most people don't see a phone contract as a credit agreement, but it is. I explained that as he was only eighteen, he had no credit history and that it was standard procedure to run a check on new customers.

He wasn't appeased and became increasingly annoyed.

"I'm not a normal customer, though," he stated indignantly. "I'm in One Direction! We were on X Factor!"

I raised an eyebrow.

"Please hold."

I pressed the red button on my phone turret and looked up.

"Anyone heard of One Direction?"

I glanced around at my colleagues, all on calls. Heads shook.

"Nope, no. Uh uh."

One of the younger girls raised her eyebrows and piped up, "I have!"

Too late, the majority vote was in.

I pressed the hold button again.

"Sorry, sir, we still have to conduct a check."

The line went dead.

A week later, we were all shocked and amused when One Direction hit the charts at Number One and was in every teen magazine on the shelves. Just think, there was I with Zayn Malik's personal details, current telephone number, home address, the lot. If I'd been a minimum-wage One Direction fan, it would have been solid gold.

I enjoyed my job in the early days. Some customers were rude and nasty, but others were lovely. Take the old man who couldn't make calls on his mobile, for example. He was so sweet. I saw from his account he was in his eighties and couldn't call his son, as he had no signal. I checked the coverage checker and could see immediately that a fault was showing for his closest cell site.

"Hello, thank you for holding. I've just had a look and I'm afraid that the closest cell site to you has a fault that is causing your issue with making calls. What I'll do is put in a request for an engineer to go out, as you've been able to make calls previously and have good coverage. It will hopefully be sorted quickly."

"Ah! Don't you bother yourself doing that, pet," he said. "I'll grab my tools and I'll pop out and have a look at it for you."

The image of this little old man turning up to fix potentially four-hundred feet of cell tower with his spanner and screwdriver set made me smile.

"That's very kind," I assured him, "but it needs an engineer with specialist equipment, I'm afraid."

"Right you are, pet, but the offers there, it'd be no trouble."

After a couple of years in sales, I applied for a promotion and was successful in joining the Debt, Fraud, and Security department. This was an eye-opener as to what happens when personal details aren't secure. It was a member of our department who had spilled the beans to the newspapers that Victoria Beckham was pregnant for the first time with their son, Brooklyn. Back then, all text messages were visible to advisors on the systems, and the individual in question had seen a text to David, from Victoria, confirming her pregnancy. They called a newspaper, hoping to get paid for the story.

When the complaint came in, the shit hit the fan! As I walked into the office that morning, it was silent. The heaviness of the atmosphere was enough to squeeze the breath out of me. Various managers were milling about, talking quietly in small huddles. All the advisors were sitting in silence at their desks with clenched bottoms, making worried eye-faces at each other. One by one, we were called into a small office at the end of the department and behind closed doors, were grilled in the manner of suspects in a murder case. It went on all day. When it was my turn, I was already a bag of nerves from just watching the others come out shaken, eyes downcast. As I sat down at the desk, I glanced at my manager and another hard-faced and sharp-suited woman from Human Resources sitting opposite. They looked like they meant business.

"You know there has been a breach of security regarding the Beckham account?"

I nodded. "Yes."

I felt hot and itchy. The interrogation began, and I answered as truthfully as I could.

"Did you log onto the Beckham account? Did you receive any calls from anyone saying they worked for the Beckhams?

What is the procedure for reading a personal text and under what circumstances would you do it?"

The questions went on and on. As I answered, I tried to arrange my facial expressions to show that I wasn't involved. I felt guilty even though I'd done nothing wrong. Last: "Do you know who read the text and sold the story?"

I shook my head emphatically.

"No."

Phew!

The next morning, every newspaper, every television channel, and every radio station had the news and were announcing the pregnancy. Pictures of Victoria Beckham were everywhere, and every hushed conversation in the office was about her. I reckon that's when she stopped smiling. Speculation as to the guilty party rumbled around the banks of desks, no one daring to talk openly about it for fear of inviting suspicion upon themselves.

Of course, the hoo-ha died down eventually, and life went on as normal. A member of staff was suddenly absent a week later and never returned, but we never found out if they were the one who had leaked the news. If they were, I hope they got paid well for the story. Not long afterwards, the updated company policy stated that only the police could apply to read text messages.

The team of people I worked with was great, but we weren't what I would call 'friends'. They were mostly older than I was, both in age and attitude. In such a large company, people would come and go. From my experience, even the ones who seemed closest would never see each other again once they'd left. We would chat, of course, but it would mostly involve complaining about the company, the managers, and the archaic and useless computer systems. We never saw each other outside of work. I tell a lie – Josh and I met a couple from my department in town for drinks a couple of times. We didn't make repeat plans, because we had nothing in common but work.

When again, desperate for friends, I found myself almost begging them to meet up for a drink, I checked myself, and saddened, gave up. It wasn't their fault any more than it was mine. I guess that somehow, they could probably sense I was a fake. I wasn't like them, but I was trying to be. I was still trying to fit in with a tribe that wasn't mine. Josh was the same, never one to be out every Friday on the piss with the lads. We had essentially become our own best friends, but for me, it wasn't enough.

Melanie taught me the funniest lesson (funny in that she thought I'd believe it). She told me solemnly that recreational drugs are "not big and not clever", and to keep a low profile about our new 'hobby'. I was like, "They bloody are clever! They're amazing!"

It's like that television series you want everyone to watch or the book you couldn't put down. You just want everyone else to have the same fantastic experience. In the honeymoon period, I just wanted to shout it from the rooftops but decided instead to tentatively hint at it to my other two children. It wasn't quite "Hey, kids, Mum has taken up dressmaking," so I was unsure how the news would go down. What I didn't expect was the eye-rolling and grinning of two of the fruit of my loins. They happily began to relay all their past ecstasy experiences as teenagers, most of which involved sneaking in the door, completely saucer-eyed, doing their best to look normal while chatting with me in the kitchen. There are none so blind – I never had a clue! To be honest, I should have known it with the likes of my family.

I've always been one to have a bash at most things to the extent that when I once decided to have a go at up-cycling,

Melanie misread my text as 'unicycling' and never batted an eyelid. She just told me to be careful I didn't fall off! Why did I think my children would be any less adventurous?

My sister, Katy, a regular user of LSD when she was in her late teens, was also open about her past usage. Again, I couldn't believe I'd never realised; but I was a mother by then, so how would I? I could sense though that she felt dismissive of me for finding recreational drugs at this age, and even now she doesn't particularly want to talk about my experiences. I try to respect that, but it's difficult sometimes to have to stilt my conversation – particularly if I've had a good night or been to an event and want to tell her about it. I quickly learnt to recognise the people I could share my discovery with, and when to keep quiet. Keeping quiet – that was a lesson for me on its own! Melanie told me in the beginning, "Be careful how much personal information you share when you're on Mandy," and she was right.

Taking into consideration that Mandy encourages connections with strangers, you can imagine some of the conversations that have arisen. If I had taken a bit too much, my blabbermouth would talk about a plethora of subjects. At a rate of knots you would hardly think possible – some serious and interesting, others absolute tripe. The wonderful thing about Mandy-infused conversations is that I know exactly what I'm talking about and am perfectly lucid. Some of my best in-depth discussions have been on Mandy. There can also be a lot of intimate oversharing, though. On a couple of occasions, I had awoken the next day with the sobering memory that I'd told my latest new 'friend' the details of my sex life, the regrets and reasons for any crimes I may have committed, and waxed both lyrical and philosophical about life and the Universe. Then, I'd stumble off to another stranger and continue my diatribe about why Teletubbies have aerials on their heads and my latest cocked-up order from 'Wish.com' (my experience was ordering a set of oil paints and receiving a Chipmunk costume as an alternative. As it happens, I've worn that costume at more events than I care to admit, so not all purchases are a disaster).

Upon reflection, it's surprising which of these conversations I would forget the next day, and which are the ones that still come back to me with hot-cheeked embarrassment. Experience and intuition eventually zipped my lips and I'm always aware of what I choose to disclose nowadays.

SESH LIFE

What a gift for a child to take a parent under their wing and welcome them into the most private part of their lives. No, not the intimate sexual one, but the part that makes them who they truly are. What a leap of trust and love that, once given, cannot be taken back again. Melanie and Robin did that for Josh and me. Possibly, had they not, we would have melted back into our usual ways with yearnings and regrets at what could have been. I'm certain that's what would have happened, as we had no other connections to guide us, and we were too shy and socially anxious to attempt to make any. We wouldn't have known where to start. Melanie, who knew me best, however, took the matter in hand.

As luck would have it, a few weeks later, a little camp-out was going on for Melanie's like-minded friends, at the home of one of her friend's parents. *Other parents? Other parents, who know Mandy?* Melanie asked them if we could gate-crash, and at the very last minute, we got an invitation. Looking back, we were shameless in turning up to a stranger's garden party, but such was our level of enthusiasm, we threw caution and humility to the wind and accepted, never guessing it would turn out to be a memorable night for many reasons.

Josh and I already knew Ally, Melanie's friend, but only in passing. We had never met her parents, Malcolm and June, who lived a few miles away in a massive house they were renovating. Josh and I had a little caravan, and it was with this we arrived at their house. *What a perfect piece of land for a party camp-out!* More than a garden, it was like a small woodland with trees and a bonfire built and ready to go. There were also a few others there – friends of Melanie and Robin's we hadn't met before. There was also Van Gav who we last saw at their house. He ambled over to Josh, who was sitting cross-legged in his poncho, staring into space.

Van Gav peered at him inquisitively for a moment before announcing: "Fucking Hell, mate. You've changed!"

In this unfamiliar garden that night, were all ages, both men and women, and none of the normal social barriers appeared to exist. I admit to being concerned that I would be looked on purely as 'Melanie's mum'. That thought made me sad, but if that was how they thought of me, the group did not make it apparent. I felt grateful for that. All welcomed us and included us in the group.

In the centre of the garden, located a long way downhill from the actual house, was a half barrel. It was filled with water, into which everyone dumped their beers, wine, and other alcoholic drinks to keep cool for the evening. Being total amateurs, Josh and I had only brought cider and beer, no water. That was a big mistake! We had no idea at the time how important it would be to be vigilant about hydration.

Melanie, Robin, and everyone else had brought their supplies in the form of small pills in a variety of pastel colours, bearing impressed designs – the instantly recognisable 'E's. And so we danced, talked, accepted more pills, sat on the grass by the roaring fire, and became dehydrated. Apart from Melanie, Robin, and Ally, we knew no one, and although everyone was quickly wide-eyed and huggy, we still had enough natural shyness left to not dare ask for any water, as it would mean a trek up to the house.

We quickly became so mellow and loved up that all was well with the world, and everyone was our best friends. This was exactly what we wanted. We were sitting, chatting, and connecting with total strangers and they were talking back! I don't recall how many pills we took, but in retrospect, it was too many. In all honesty, I remember taking only one and feeling that rush of euphoria, but I know top-ups were freely handed out, and I accepted every time. Before I knew it, my eyes were dancing, my body was vibrating, and I was clenching my jaw, which I recognised from the last time we had Mandy. This is one of the issues with Mandy. You become so mellow and happy that a little more every so often is simply keeping the love going.

At some point during the night, we were all sitting in a bizarre conga-type line on the grass. One of the men suggested we all take our tops off. I thought nothing of it, but don't be fooled by the hedonistic vibe that accompanies rolling on Mandy. I was sitting behind Ally's dad, stroking his head and shoulders and losing myself in the sensory experience. Josh was sitting somewhere near with his shirt off, something he never does in public, and the whole air bristled with expectation. Melanie, however, a veteran of this kind of situation, was on the ball, and thank goodness she was.

"Errrr, no!" she said firmly. "No one is taking their tops off."

Would I have done it had she not stepped in? Probably, if everyone else had. I also know I'd have died a million deaths of embarrassment thereafter, too. Mandy has a very mischievous side, and I have to be very aware of doing embarrassing things I may come to regret later.

By dawn the next morning, we were so deficient in liquid that we were practically desiccated. Having had no water, no sleep, and way too much Mandy, we felt ill. Arriving home with crippling headaches and aching bodies, we resolved to 'take more water with it' in the future. Lack of water can be extremely dangerous when on Mandy, so we were very lucky we had escaped a far worse side effect.

It took days to recover from that night. Lots of sleep, though, and we were ready for the next exciting event. I was in the honeymoon period and just couldn't wait to do it again.

Some at parties think nothing of pushing their boundaries or those of their relationships. If you're single, or a swinger, who cares, right? We are neither. I realised I had enjoyed the skin contact with Ally's dad, but why? I hadn't fancied him, but had I subconsciously hoped he'd fancy me? Maybe it was the old me surfacing? Was I pushing our relationship boundaries because I knew that on Mandy I could get away with it? Maybe it was all or none of those things. Josh and I talked about it later and he said he felt aware and slightly uncomfortable about the way I behaved, and that alone was enough to make me take a step back and become my own observer. The very fact I was questioning myself meant I needed to remember that Mandy is my teacher, not a cheeky mate, egging me on. If I occasionally find my inebriated self attempting to justify my behaviour to my sober self, I pause and ask the questions again.

I have witnessed people acting out of character (or perhaps indulging their actual character) whilst using Mandy and socially vulnerable individuals being exploited. Now, before I go any further, this doesn't mean sexual exploitation. It's more of a sensual dropping of the guard. I know I was ripe for it – wanting friends, low self-esteem, awkward in large social groups. If I spotted anyone who wanted a hug or who I sensed I could cuddle up to, I was there with bells on. Now I have a few experiences under my belt, I can sense who to approach for the more 'sensual' aspect of the event and whom not to.

This exploitation isn't intentional, but the more vulnerable people are the ones that the more aware people will push their luck with. It's strange how Mandy taught me about connection but now allowed me to put those lessons into practice on my own. I no longer feel the need to sit on the laps of strange men or cuddle up to a lot of my female friends at a gathering. I'm aware enough on Mandy to ask a stranger if they are comfortable with hugs instead of launching myself at them.

It's a wonderful feeling to now just sit and talk calmly with people I feel are friends, whilst also being able to engage easily with strangers.

Although I felt the benefit from Mandy immediately, the first few times I sometimes felt confused and rejected once the affection and bonds of the evening were replaced by reality the next day. Josh and I have found that even when we are peaking, we still have a clarity of thought that enables us to be aware of the situation we are in, and the people around us. I know where Josh is, and he knows where I am. I would still feel uncomfortable cuddling up to some people, knowing that their partners may not be at ease with it. This clarity is one of the many benefits of the 'love drug'. I was also aware that I shouldn't give Melanie and Robin cause for concern that we might act daft and show them up. Dosage and intention are the bottom lines. One thing I noticed is that the same dosage affects everyone differently and I see this in the regular group we tend to meet up with. It's funny because even though I'm wide-eyed and high on Mandy, I can recognise those same signs in someone I'm talking to as if I were completely sober. This is clear with psychedelics such as LSD too, which I'll come to later.

SAGE AND HORROR

As a new Mandy user, I quickly became concerned about an additional problem I had never considered. Where do I hide the stuff? On our way to festivals, I'd shoved a couple of pills in the toes of my flat pumps. This was a brilliant idea to me. No stacked heels to cause suspicion, and a few steps of 'ouch' toes aren't exactly a hardship when you walk straight through and into anywhere. Oh, how smug I was.

The following year after our introduction to Mandy, we went on holiday to my favourite place – Turkey. Each year Josh and I go to the same hotel, which hosts an evening of traditional song and dance. Every time, without fail, I spend months before this holiday learning a different Turkish folk song. I sing it, read the lyrics, record and listen to it, and sing it again every single day to perfect my performance in preparation. On the night, I hand in a bit of paper with my name written on it, for essentially the most bizarre karaoke session you could witness. I often used to wonder why I am so drawn to doing things I know make me feel anxious, for attention and admiration, but in examining my relationship with my parents,

I now understand why. You'd think that insight would have cured the compulsion, but no.

This holiday was no different. I sat, downing a strong, neon-coloured all-inclusive cocktail, shaking with fear. My legs were wobbling so much that I could barely make it to the stool, which was in the view of a hundred or so inebriated and cheering holidaymakers. It's a good job I had a tan, but I could even feel that sliding off my face, which must have shown up drip white in the blazing lights. Surrounding by hooting and tambourine-bashing dancers, spinning and whirling around the stage, I opened my mouth. The music started, the lights flashed and went crazy, and then out it came.

The song exploded from me like I was vomiting out a legion of demons, all shrieking in tongues in the darkness. I made no eye contact with the audience, even though I knew Josh was somewhere out there, smiling with encouragement. If I could just keep the words coming in the correct tune and order, I'd get to the end and be fine. The last line of the song was a mixture of melody and a shuddering breath of pure relief, as I realised I'd come through unscathed, and everyone was clapping and cheering. I allowed myself a smile, and amid the noise, returned to my seat. *That was fun, eh?* Nope, it was bloody terrifying. My stomach was still churning with nerves, but you could bet that the following year I'd do it again. My very grounding and sensible friend Dawn astutely points out that I'm working on the principle that if I go first, I can't be put off by the experiences of anyone following. That ensures I keep the time I am consumed by my fear to a minimum. However, the reality of always 'going first' hasn't always worked out in my favour, but I digress.

Back in the airport, ready to fly home, my suitcase was rammed like a Jenga game, with boxes of pairs of fake designer shoes. Converse and Vans for the family and UGG slippers for me. It's no problem bringing back eleven pairs of shoes; after all, it's the biggest tourist purchase in Turkey. We had a great week before heading back home.

Luggage checked in, we sat and ate tasteless and expensive airport snacks and half-dozed until our gate was called. The queue moved quickly, and Josh went through to wait for me on the other side. A Turkish border control woman asked me in halting, broken English to pop my bag on the shelf. She was small with black hair tied back under a peaked cap and dressed entirely in a crisp black uniform, from the trousers of which dangled various implements of restraint. Her 'don't mess with me' expression froze me into compliance immediately. There was no problem; she was surely just doing her job, as I knew I had only my purse and half a Kit-Kat in there.

"Please put your arms out at shoulder level," she said, demonstrating.

I smiled what I hoped was a winning smile at her and did as she asked. She ran her scanner over me with a face like a smacked arse.

"I now do legs, stand apart slightly."

I stepped my feet apart, and she scanned my body and legs down to my feet… and it all kicked off.

BEEP!

The scanner emitted a shrieking alarm and a light on the top flashed red. The woman looked up at me sharply and then waved the scanner over my other foot.

BEEEEEEP!

I was rigid with horror. I knew for sure this must be an error, but she wasn't having any of it. In my panic, I leaned over, grabbed my bag, and tipped the whole contents onto the table to prove I was innocent of whatever the alarm was detecting.

"Look, that's everything," I garbled at her

"Here, here!" snapped the woman at a male security officer, who immediately hurried over.

Similarly attired and complete with a solid-looking cosh and gun, this guy looked narrow-eyed and menacing. Other passengers in the queue backed away slightly. I looked around in a panic. I caught Josh's eye over the other side and made an "I'm innocent, honest!" face at him.

Well, these two officers jabbered away at each other for a minute before taking the scanner to a drug testing machine. I strained to see what it showed on the screen. A moment later, it flashed red for ecstasy, but I had none. I hadn't taken any, but I swear for a few moments there was a distinct possibility I'd poo my pants right there and then. I've seen the television series, *Banged up Abroad*. I was already crying inside at the thought of being a crazed criminal's bitch, and the embassy not listening to the pleas and petitions of my distraught family back home.

They waved the scanner again, and the machine was like, 'Are you blind? It's RED. Lock her up. She's a drug mule!' My stomach felt like it had rats running races around inside. I was bloody terrified. Suddenly the woman jabbered something at the man, waved wildly at me, and snapped, "You go!"

I went. I've never gone as fast anywhere in my life. Scooping up my bag and bits in one fluid movement, Kit Kat falling to the floor and abandoned, I scrambled across to the other side. Josh hadn't been able to see everything that had gone on. He was smirking and found it quite funny.

"Ha, laugh now, Josh! You wouldn't have been laughing if I'd been in prison, you jerk."

I was shaking for a good while after.

On the plane later, very quietly, we discussed what must have happened. The shoes I was wearing were the super comfy, ancient, and somewhat aromatic pumps I'd stored my pills in previously. It seemed there was still enough residue to alert the scanner. Such a simple explanation and probably why they let me off so easily, as it was clear there was nowhere to hide the pills in such flat shoes (except I *had* done so before). Had it alerted them to anywhere else on my body, I'd probably have ended up frog-marched to a back room equipped with a box of rubber gloves and a tube of lube.

We were a bit giddy. Mandy was our new friend, but one we were completely reliant on Robin and Melanie for. It seems silly, but initially, we didn't dare to ask them for it in case they thought we were too excitable and getting in over our heads. In our many discussions on how Mandy had benefited us, the subject of Ayahuasca had often come up. Ayahuasca is a traditional spiritual plant medicine, used for many centuries by the tribes in the Amazon. It was used in ceremonies to release negativity and answer the many questions human beings have about life and existence. We were fascinated by this, but as traditional ceremonies were financially beyond our reach, we looked at cheaper and more accessible alternatives.

I thought about my teenage past and a holiday in Amsterdam where many plant medicines and soft drugs are still legal. Josh and I discussed ordering some magic mushrooms or truffles. It was nowhere near shroom season in England, so picking our own wasn't an option. Plus, I didn't feel at all comfortable in our ability to identify the right ones and escape ending up retching and semi-conscious in A&E. I did a quick internet search and a few moments later we had a twenty-gram bag of Atlantis truffles on the way. *Very natural, so can't be too bad, eh?* A week of anticipation and staking out the letterbox later, the truffles arrived in a flat, unmarked box. We were good to go. The next day was warm, so we decided we'd experience our truffle trip in the garden.

We'd looked at various ways to consume truffles and decided to grind them up, add hot water and make a kind of tea/soup. Josh dislikes mushrooms in any form, so it seemed a good option – swill it down fast and hardly taste it. That was the plan, anyway. The truffles weren't at all dry as we had expected; they were moist and spongy and resembled something akin to a tumorous growth. They also smelled disgusting. No way could we grind these things, so we mashed them as best we could with a variety of cutlery, pouring hot water on top.

Now, if you've ever had an accidental bit of eggshell in your mouth, you'll know that the more you chew it, the more it breaks up and increases in volume until it seems your entire mouth is full of it. Well, that's like truffles. Sitting in the sun outside, we drank the foul grey liquid, which left most of the mashed-up truffles brown and claggy in the bottom of our cups. We looked at each other doubtfully and scooped them out with our fingers, poking the mush into our mouths. We chewed and gagged, our eyes watering at the awfulness of the ordeal. After way too long, we swallowed the stinking, revolting gloop down. We sat and waited, we discussed the neighbours, our day, everything, all the while waiting for… well, anything. Nothing happened, absolutely nothing. Josh said it appeared that colours seemed sharper and clearer, but it could just have been wishful thinking, as he was squinting a bit in the sun. I squinted a bit too, hoping that perhaps you could only see Truffle-Heaven through one eye. *Well, you never know.*

What a waste of time and money. After a couple of hours, we went inside and watched a film on television, vowing not to bother with truffles again. Back to the drawing board. We looked again at medicinal plants, noticing one we recognised the name of. It had a similar effect to Ayahuasca but with a shorter duration. Feeling encouraged, we placed an order for Salvia Divinorum (of the sage family of plants) from a website with a high rate of easy deliveries. What could go wrong?

It went wrong so completely and utterly that even now, we still laugh at our collective naivety, and what unfolded from the moment we placed the order. Melanie was also interested in Salvia, as the effect was supposed to be remarkably similar to that of Ayahuasca. The following week, a flat box with a Netherlands stamp slid through our letterbox. We were so excited that we ripped the box open, scattering leaflets from inside it all over the floor. *Leaflets?* We shook the mutilated box upside down, rifled through the advertising bumf and stock list, and realisation dawned. We'd been robbed! Our illegal, but legitimately paid-for stash of drugs had been swiped. In our eagerness to open the box, it had escaped our notice that it wasn't sealed in the first place. No tape, no glue, it just slotted together, and some arsehole en route had nicked our stuff. We were so disappointed. Sixty quid had gone west and all we had to show for it was an empty box and slumped spirits. I was furious, but it's not like we could complain to the police. However, what I love about Josh and me is our joint stoicism. We complained to the company who we had ordered from, and astonishingly, they agreed to resend our order.

The second package arrived with no problems. Delighted by the success of our bags of Salvia stashed safely in the kitchen cupboard, and with a newly purchased bong on its way, we reconsidered the truffles. In the face of all adversity, we decided to give it another shot. Josh searched the internet and figured we hadn't had enough, so we made a larger order. This time we bought fifty grams.

Another wait ensued. We waited and waited. As we waited, we checked posts on the Internet. Overall, people thought that if we'd been waiting over two weeks, our package had almost certainly been intercepted by Border Control. If that happened to be the case, we'd likely receive a sharply worded letter warning us to grow up and not do it again. *Not too bad.* It was typical though – another waste of money! A month later, no letter had arrived, and we were just happy we'd got off lightly. We decided not to potentially lose any more cash by sending it abroad and agreed to forget about truffles. They tasted horrible, anyway.

One evening we were happily vegging on the sofa, watching telly, when the doorbell rang. We weren't expecting anyone. More than likely, it would be Amazon delivering the guitar bits and pieces that turn up every other week for Josh. He was nearest the door, so I let him go while I carried on watching *Emmerdale*. I think it was a few moments before I realised Josh was still at the door, so I got up and looked out of the window. I swear the police van parked across the road was a riot van. No little cop car for our one transgression – no, sir! We got the full effect and so did the neighbours – a massive black police van and a uniformed officer who looked like a cross between the Terminator and a strippergram standing on our front porch.

Oh my God! Oh my God! I hopped around in the living room panicking for a moment, before taking my courage in both hands, somehow my mouth too, and rushing to join in the fray. I ran into the hallway and saw Josh – drip white and mumbling something illegible at the stern-looking giant of a cop. He was reading from his notepad about "An order of illegal magic truffles". He raised his eyebrows at us from under his cap.

"Well?"

It was like the Spartacus movie. I had to save my loved one!

"It was me!" I squeaked, my voice cracking, then louder. "It was me! I ordered the truffles; he knew nothing about it. I never told him, honest."

I gesticulated wildly at Josh, who looked close to fainting on the spot. The copper reared back slightly as I blathered out my gibberish and high-pitched squawking version of a confession. I reckon if he'd had a taser, his hand would have been twitching on it just in case I truly was dangerous and insane. I became increasingly and horrifically aware of the open house door behind me, and the policeman's direct eye-view of our newly arrived bong, which was sitting on the kitchen worktop.

What if the policeman called for backup and we got raided? We had Salvia and Mandy in the cupboard and were not the nice middle-class couple we appeared to be at all. I got a faint whiff of weed from next door but one. Hopping and shuffling around, grinning manically, I hoped I could obscure his view and appear innocent and gormless. What a trio we were – Josh apologising profusely, the copper getting through his legal obligation by reading his 'telling off' script as fast as possible, so he could escape this madhouse, and me jigging about around them both. In an attempt to lighten the mood and help bring the whole palaver to its conclusion, I spouted cheekily (and I hoped appealingly), "Well, that's us smacked, then!"

Wrong choice of words. I gave up. I'm a useless criminal. On balance, however, I reckon I'm probably one of the bravest cowards I know. Even the cop allowed himself a small grin. We must have looked like the most unlikely pair of drug dealers the law has ever confronted. I had my counterfeit Turkish fluffy slippers and dressing gown on, and I was way too comfy and suburban-looking to be a big player in the drugs war. Seriously though, all that fuss and drama for only fifty grams of truffles! Once the cop had departed, Josh quickly logged on to the laptop and updated the internet know-it-alls about our ordeal.

We invited Melanie and Robin over that weekend to try the Salvia. We were going to smoke it. It looks like little dried flakes of parsley (well, it is a type of sage after all), and has hardly any smell. Anyone who didn't know would assume it was weed. It comes in extract strengths of 10x, 20x, and up to

30x the strength of the raw leaf, which is traditionally chewed. Josh had been researching the protocol for smoking Salvia and had found a website that stated the calculations and dosage information for beginners.

We were thrilled that we had maybe discovered another 'medicine' as wonderful and nurturing as Mandy. Josh was in the kitchen with his scales-of-dubious-accuracy from Amazon. Melanie, Robin, and I were all animated and nattering away in our living room. One of us bright sparks suggested that Robin film our experiences so we could watch them back later. Robin is nervous about psychedelics, and he likes to stay in control, so he was the obvious candidate. If Mandy was amazing, this was going to be next level, and next level it was! In came Josh with the water bong (which fortunately hadn't been spotted by the policeman a couple of weeks earlier), which cools the smoke before inhalation. It's a giant of a thing and was bought on the basis that the bigger the item, the more of a bargain it is.

"Ooooooooooooh" we all intoned, watching as Josh sprinkled the measured flakes of Salvia into the bong. Like in Turkey with the karaoke, I had already fought my way to going first by pulling rank as Mother, householder, and resident idiot. With the camera rolling, Josh passed the bong to me.

"Okay, when I light the Salvia, wait a moment until the chamber of the bong fills with smoke. Inhale it all smoothly, hold it in as long as you can, then breathe out."

"Yep, got it." I nodded, nervously.

Robin and Melanie were comfy on the sofa; they were sitting like a pair of kids watching a Disney movie, grinning away happily… until the poisoned apple is handed to Snow White, of course.

It was easy – no harsh smoke, no coughing, just a nice smooth inhale and hold, exactly as Josh had instructed.

"Ah yeah." I sighed, smiling at my audience.

They smiled back encouragingly.

"Yeah, I can definitely feel someth—"

Thank God there had been a footstool next to me because I face-planted it. I didn't move other than to scream in abject and guttural terror for the next ten minutes without pausing for breath. Bless Robin – as our sitter, he was superb. He was on the video, murmuring comfortingly to a horrified Josh and Melanie that "she's having a good time".

I was not having a good time. I was being tipped head-first over and over into hell. It was the blackest, deepest pit of eternal terror. I was there forever; I wasn't even me!

Afterwards, everyone asked, "What did you see?"

The truth is, I saw nothing, because in the horror I was trapped in, I had no eyes, I had no head; I didn't even have a body at all, which made me completely incapable of moving. I hadn't been conscious of what was happening, or the presence of anyone else in the room. I was just my brain, trapped, pitching forward over and over and over in a never-ending nightmare of blackness. I can only describe it as clinging to a cliff edge by your fingernails and then falling into the chasm for all eternity. I remember the blackness wearing off, though. I could hear my screams. Gradually, I could move one arm and raise myself off the footstool, although it felt like I was clawing myself away from the imaginary pit edge. After sitting up, I could see and talk to the others, but in the immediate aftermath, I had no recollection of smoking Salvia at all. For a second or two, I was confused as to why my family members were in our house, looking so traumatised. Watching the video back later was jaw-dropping. I had gone down like a bloody rock. My screams were so loud and terrified that Melanie expressed wide-eyed concern about the neighbours hearing and calling the police. As it wore off, though, I was laughing and excited about what had happened. It made no sense at all. I can only relate it to like being in shock. Looking back, I'm astonished I didn't die of fear. It's surely got to be possible, hasn't it?

You know when they say, 'The apple doesn't fall far from the tree'? Well, cue idiot number two. Why on earth when I came round it wasn't to Robin and Melanie screeching tyres and churning gravel, speeding away to safety, I still don't know, but Melanie was all, "Me next", completely happy to follow the Pied Piper into purgatory. She decided to lie down, which after my experience was the one sensible move she made. Her experience with Salvia couldn't have been more different. Smoking her bong, she grinned happily and started laughing with what appeared genuine joy as she berated Robin with one expletive after another. She was so hilarious that it was hard not to laugh out loud and break whatever spell she was under. Her arms stuck out in all directions as she rolled toward the back of the sofa, being pushed by some unseen force stronger than herself.

"Oh, great!" she laughed wryly. "Now I'm a tube of Fruit Pastilles."

Fruit Pastilles? She was talking away, telling in a confused but happy rambling that she was now turning into the letters A and R and her arms were forming the letter shapes. For the whole duration of her trip, she was laughing at, and abusing, poor Robin, who was bemused and didn't seem sure whether she was serious or not. Thank goodness we filmed this stuff. It's drugs and comedy gold and a real-time cautionary tale. Melanie's experience, however, indicated something else about her, which would arise again much later, and with a far different recreational drugs experiment.

Josh is naturally more cautious by nature than me, but he wasn't being left behind on this! He sat on the sofa, lit the bong, took the full hit in one, and passed it quickly to me. What followed was completely bizarre. He was so wide-eyed you could tell that there was no one at home in his head. He recalls the experience as:

"I laid down on the sofa and within five seconds my arms were waving all over the place. I could see myself from above, lying down (the roof of the house was gone). Suddenly I fell right through the sofa and landed on the old sofa in my parents' house, over a hundred and eighty miles away. I could see a man with a beard and glasses talking to me, but all I could see were his lips moving. I couldn't hear him at all."

Wow. This was freaky as hell to listen to.

"Did you recognise the man?" I probed gently.

"No, he seemed far away. He didn't seem to want to come closer to me," Josh muttered. I could see his mind working overtime to process what he'd seen.

"The room then melted and swirled in rainbow colours, like sweets. I felt I was rolling with the swirl, trying to stop it, but my skin was sloughing away from my arms. Thomas the Tank Engine's face appeared on a Yule Log, and he also rolled around and melted into a coloured lollipop."

The three of us stared at him, open-mouthed at what we were hearing. This was different again from either Melanie's or my experience. I wondered vaguely where these visions came from.

"The whole bungalow melted again, and I saw yours and Melanie's faces. I focused as best I could and as I got closer, I fell away and melted into a kind of swirly cake icing and the faces wobbled around on red stalks. I turned away (as well as a swirl of icing can) and watched a giant spider doing 'jazz hands' at me."

It was amusing how so much of Josh's experience was focused on sweets, cakes, and lollipops. We encouraged him to go on.

"I saw flowers in the room, and I now saw Big Bird from Sesame Street before he also swirled away. Then, I started to come around. My vision was very weird, kind of like a pinhole where the centre was reality, and the peripheral was still my parent's bungalow. As I shook my arms and legs, coming out of the trip, my reality got bigger until I was back in the room."

"Whoa!" we all chorused in disbelief. We fell silent for a moment, unsure what to say.

"Never, ever will I do this again!" he finished emphatically.

What had happened was that Josh got up from the sofa. This was quite alarming, as he's a big bloke, and had he dived out of a glass window, we'd have been powerless to apprehend him. His eyes were wide and unseeing and, fortunately, after a moment, he slumped into a sitting position on the floor. He pointed happily and chatted in a very effeminate way with Big Bird from Sesame Street and the spider. We tried not to laugh, as, although it was hilarious, we could also have incorporated our response into his trip. He seemed happy but confused about coming around. Unlike Melanie, there was almost no sign that he was conscious of us in the room with him. What we *did* all agree, however, is that we had smoked too much, we were terrified out of our wits at the total loss of control, glad we'd had the experience just so that we knew what it was like, and that we had made it through still compos mentis.

Josh and I still have two full bags of Salvia, untouched in our cupboard, where they will remain for the foreseeable future. They will serve as a warning if we get too blasé about trying anything else. Again, it's all about boundaries and dosage. If you can't control those, don't do drugs, kids! On the upside, we still smile mischievously at the thought of the thief who nicked our first package of Salvia. We can picture him congratulating himself on his free weed as he settled down for a smoke and a chilled-out evening. You just gotta love Karma!

I discovered very early in our meetings with Mandy that I could go to bed after a good evening and return to the coming-up feeling for many days afterwards. I would close my eyes and simply think back to the sensation, and there it would be. It's a wonderful thing, but useless as I'm a talker when rolling, not a sleeper. Therefore, I find that the euphoria keeps me awake all night. The ability fades after a few days and disappears. I'm guessing that it's the natural high I feel when taking Mandy, combined with the human connection, which is so special to me, that mentally I'm loath to let it go.

I'm one of those people that got pregnant and bought every *Mother and Baby* magazine published. I took up painting and followed over twenty Facebook groups connected with art. I've always been like a giant sponge, soaking up information about every subject that interests me, and Mandy was no exception. The search bar of my YouTube history displayed every episode of *Drugs Lab* ever released. The Dutch government funded the programme as a response to the number of young people taking illegal drugs (with a few class-A exceptions such as heroin and methamphetamine, which are most definitely not what I'd call recreational). Three presenters who appeal to a young to mid-twenties age group would take drugs, live on television, so that the viewer was able to see how the drug affected them. As an idea, it seems bizarre, but educationally it's invaluable and extremely entertaining. I would recommend watching it to anyone interested in learning about drugs for any reason.

Working our way through every episode, Josh and I would watch the presenters take MDMA, magic mushrooms, speed, and DMT. *Ooh, DMT!* Our ears would prick up whenever it was mentioned. Like Mandy, we had heard that it had the effect of joy and enlightenment we were drawn to, with the added benefit that we could extract it ourselves. The reaction to this drug, which is smoked, has a profoundly positive and spiritual effect lasting no longer than fifteen minutes or so and has no hangover period, which appealed to us. The chemical name, N,N-Dimethltryptamine is believed to be naturally present in plants, animals, and humans and is the reason some people have near-death experiences. It is secreted by the pineal gland at birth, death, and during lucid dream states.

Now, before I go any further, please be assured that Mandy is not a 'gateway' drug for other harder and more dangerous drugs. You won't find people slumped glassy-eyed on benches from using most recreational drugs. The key is the word 'recreational'. Whilst Mandy was difficult to obtain, unless from Robin, we could make DMT in our kitchen, from legally acquired ingredients. *How convenient.*

PITFALLS

We were a few months on from the Salvia experiment, and although a little more cautious, still interested in plant medicines. It wasn't that Mandy wasn't enough, I think it was simply curiosity that had been released into the light like the opening of Pandora's Box. Melanie and Robin popped in unannounced for a cuppa one weekend en route to see Baz, one of Robin's old friends. They knew each other from the music scene and had decided to get together for a catch-up. Josh and I had spent a few weeks on forums researching and ordering from various online stores, and our very first batch of DMT was stewing away in jars on our kitchen worktop. It all looked very scientific and complicated (it isn't – every science experiment I ever did at school failed, so if it had been we wouldn't have bothered, simple). We hadn't told Melanie and Robin that we were having a go at making some, so they were both surprised and, I suspect, a tad impressed, especially as neither of them had ever tried it either. After inspecting the jars and shaking their heads, with puzzled smiles and big hugs, off they went, muttering to each other that it was like a scene from *Breaking Bad*. Melanie phoned me later from Baz's house.

"You will NOT believe this, Mum, but you know all that DMT stuff in your kitchen? Well, there's the same lot of paraphernalia on Baz's kitchen worktop! He's making DMT as well! What are the chances of that?"

I was as surprised as she was and delighted when she said that Baz and his girlfriend Poppy had offered to come to our house to facilitate our first DMT ceremony the following weekend. I couldn't get out fast enough how much we'd love that. *Connection!* There were other people like us, and they wanted to spend time with us, too! I was over the moon and couldn't stop talking about it. I couldn't wait for the weekend.

After what seemed like a year of waiting in anticipation and excitement, Saturday arrived. We spent all day tidying up and shopping for orange juice, bread, eggs, waffles, and other stuff for the morning after. Impulsively, we had invited Baz and Poppy to stay at ours, and Melanie and Robin would be parking their vintage orange VW Campervan at the top of our garden and staying over too. Reminding myself that this was the new me, I resisted the almost overwhelming temptation to tie our wardrobe handles together and lock our valuables away in case they would nick our stuff. Well, we didn't know them from Adam, and you never know, do you?

Around seven that evening, we got a text to say Baz and Poppy were about five minutes away. It was November and already dark outside. They would be due to arrive around the same time as Melanie and Robin. Baz and Poppy would be parking around the front of the house, and we'd left our back gates open for Melanie and Robin's van.

A few minutes after seven, we heard their van pull up. We jumped up from the sofa and nervously started down the stone front steps to meet this mysterious couple for the first time. Josh reached out to shake the hand of the Jesus-in-cargo-shorts character that stood before us. Smiling shyly, Baz appeared to be in his mid-thirties, tall and slim with kind eyes and had a well-cultivated, frizzy beard. His waist-length loosely tied-back hair gave him a typical hippie vibe, and he had an instantly calming demeanour to match. I liked him immediately.

"Hi!" I greeted him, instinctively moving in for a hug, which he warmly returned. "Lovely to see you, and you too, Poppy."

Poppy was the opposite of Baz. Her flawless, line-free skin gave away her twenty-something age, and her small, fragile-looking frame seemed to flutter about in an almost childlike way. In contrast to Baz, she was smartly dressed and seemed more suited to a casual interview than an illegal drugs ceremony. Poppy's only nod to the theme of the evening was a garland of small daisies on the top of her head, drawing attention to her bum-length, wavy black hair. Her strength and confidence were hinted at in her firm hug, and the easy smile she broke into as we led them both up the steps, into the warmth of our kitchen.

A second later, the door flew open with a bang. Startled by the sudden noise, we all parted as Melanie burst into the kitchen, grinning,

"Oh, my fucking God," she half-laughed, half-screeched, over and over. She was immediately followed by Robin, who looked agitated and uncharacteristically annoyed.

"Sod off, babe, it's not funny!"

As he jigged about, the bohemian poncho he'd worn especially for the occasion flapped and whirled around him.

"For fuck's sake!!"

Josh, Poppy, Baz, and I stood still, like the supporting actors in a sitcom – bemused, but ready to join in on the action if needed. With Melanie still howling with laughter, and Robin 'fuck-fuck-fuck'ing and striding about the kitchen looking angry and upset, we surmised that their camper van had somehow ended up in a deep pit at the end of our new neighbour's back garden.

Andy is an easy-going hipster guy who moved into the house next door a few months ago and had decided to get the garden tidied up and demolish the unsightly and derelict garage. The pit had been left exposed, ready to fill, and the broken old gates had been taken away. We'd seen Andy pop out earlier, probably for a few well-earned pints.

Between gales of laughter and indignant expletives from Robin, Melanie explained that as they were driving up the back lane to our house, Robin spotted the open gateway and proudly reversed the van into the garden. telling Melanie, (who avoids reversing like the plague), "Stop fretting, babe! I could reverse this van into spaces tighter than this with one eye closed."

Suddenly, the camper lurched violently to one side and Melanie was thrown sideways.

"What the?" Robin peered out of the steeply tilted side window into the gloom.

"We've fallen down a hole!"

The van had been back-wheeled into the exposed garage pit… next door.

"Oh God, babe, it's not even your mum's house!" said Robin, panicked. "Quick, go get some help!"

Melanie, breathless with laughter, scrambled out of the wonky door and managed to find her way in the dark around the back, tripping and stumbling down the lane, and around to our house.

We all stood around for a minute, looking worriedly at each other and wondering what the best course of action would be. The worst-case scenario was that the camper would be damaged beyond repair, and our planned ceremony would be cancelled. Try telling that to Melanie, however – she was still wheezing with laughter and grinning in a manner totally inappropriate to the situation. I was just glad it wasn't Mrs Cartwright's house. She'd have had a heart attack for sure.

Josh, as usual, rose to the challenge.

"I know; I'll call Andy and explain what's happened, and then we'll see if we can all lift the back of the van. Maybe you could drive it out?" He nodded at Robin. "It can't be that heavy, and there are three of us."

Poppy, Melanie, and I agreed enthusiastically, relieved at not being included in the unlikely rescue team.

We girls stayed in the kitchen with the door open, watching. We could hear Josh in the darkness talking to Andy on the phone. There were a lot of "Don't worry", "It's not a problem", and "Okie Dokies", going on. I'll give Josh one thing – he's priceless in an emergency. His calm Queen's English southern accent would lull people in even the direst of situations into a false sense of security. I eavesdropped from the kitchen as Josh continued to reassure Andy.

"A photo? Errr yes, of course, hang on."

Andy wanted a photo of the scene to show to his mates in the pub, who thought he was having them on, and who could blame them? "There's a bright orange camper in my pit with three hippies attempting to lift it out", is quite a conversation stopper after all.

Andy returned home as quickly as he could to monitor how things were going. I would have done the same if I'd been him and an Italian Job scene was unfolding in *my* garden. Fortunately, even though it was November, it was dry out, so the guys didn't get muddy as they stood in the pit, grunting, heaving, and yelling instructions at each other as Robin started the engine. The situation looked hopeless for a while, but suddenly there was a "Go, go, GO!" and "It's out!" The van shot forwards and stopped, juddering a few feet from the pit edge. Other than a slightly crumpled back corner, it was unscathed. The collective sigh of relief from both Andy's garden and us in the kitchen misted the night air. Panic over. As we were...

With the camper safely parked in the correct garden and with all four wheels on the ground, we began our evening. Poppy had brought what I can only describe as a travelling altar with her. It was like Mary Poppins' carpet bag – seemingly bottomless. Out came candles, incense sticks, and little Buddha figurines. Then came flowers, Tarot cards, bundles of sage, tiny gold elephants, and more incense cones with little ceramic holders. It went on and on. She arranged all this paraphernalia, in some kind of order, on a little side table, and then lit the candles. Taking one of the sage bundles, she lit the end and started waving it around us, uttering a cleansing spell and filling the room with fragrant smoke. The rest of us were completely mesmerised and just let her get on with it. The past hour had been surreal, and we were ready to accept pretty much anything at that point. We all sat on the floor on cushions and blankets, which I had scattered around the floor earlier, and Baz put on a meditation video from YouTube on his mobile phone.

"Let's all close our eyes and repeat the mantra," Baz instructed, pressing the play button.

Beautiful and calming meditation music chimed through the surround sound, filling the room. A deep male voice intoned, "I am not the body; I am not even the mind."

We all solemnly repeated his words. We must have repeated the phrase over a hundred times. I sneaked a peek at the others. Josh was looking uncomfortable on his cushion.

"I am not the body; I am not even the mind."

On we all droned. I was beginning to wish I wasn't my body. My back ached, my legs hurt, and I didn't feel at all relaxed and Zen. *Get on with it, already!* At long last, after a final "Namaste", the phone guru shut up, and it was time for the night to get real. Real. Oh, the irony!

Baz asked who wanted to go first and, true to form, with the horrific Salvia experience pushed firmly to the back of my mind, I volunteered. I lay down on the floor on a blanket and Baz brought out a small glass pipe with a bowl at the end, which would house the DMT. The room was full of tension and expectation. I smiled nervously at everyone else, now silent and focused, as if watching some dangerous experiment. I raised myself onto one elbow and watched Baz tip a small amount of the yellowish powder into the bowl of the pipe.

"Okay," said Baz, smiling. "I'm going to hold the pipe and heat the DMT in the bowl. Once the vapour is in the stem, I'll put the pipe to your lips, and you inhale smoothly. It might taste a bit harsh, so be prepared. Hold it in as long as you can, then let it out. I'll then pass you another. Keep going as long as you can, then lie back and close your eyes."

It sounded simple enough.

"Okay." I nodded. "I'm ready."

I glanced around. Poppy, Josh, and Melanie smiled reassuringly back at me. Baz smiled again and held a lighter under the pipe. I watched closely as the smoke swirled into the bowl.

"Okay, here's the first," said Baz as he held the pipe to my lips. I did exactly as he had instructed. The room was silent apart from the faint sizzle of the pipe and my draw of breath. The taste was acrid, but not unbearable. I held the smoke for as long as I could, then breathed out.

"Next one," Baz instructed as he held the pipe out to me again.

It was strange. I felt slightly trembly, but nothing more than that. I took the second pull, held it, and breathed out. *Oh!* Now I could feel it. I could see fast-moving colours flashing and spinning in my vision and a high-pitched squealing noise like a Catherine Wheel on bonfire night. I felt I was wobbling and vibrating all over. I wanted to lie down but couldn't move from my raised elbow position on my own. Baz was there again with the pipe. I could just about feel it on my lips, but couldn't make out his face anymore. I shakily drew in the smoke, and, with the last mammoth effort of mind and body, I closed my eyes and lay down.

What happened next is what I can remember. I'm sure I have forgotten much more, but suddenly it was as if I *was* the vibrations; they shot me at tremendous speed into an enormous world of colour, and the feeling of rushing headlong into the unknown was overwhelming. Aware I was there, I could almost think consciously. I tried to look around, but the place I now inhabited continued to move in a spinning tunnel of purples, pinks, and colours I cannot describe, even now, as we don't have words for them. It felt like being trapped in a cartoon in the way you imagine as a child. I couldn't feel any threat and I wasn't exactly afraid – more nervous, I think. In the DMT world, I looked straight ahead into the moving shapes and colours. Gripping the blanket on either side of myself in the real world, I tried to slow down the overwhelming rushing feeling, anchoring myself into the only reality I knew. Still, I couldn't look to either side of the tunnel of colour. I could make out little figures, like hieroglyphs, dancing in the patterns, but ignoring my presence. I sensed that if I looked to either side, I would feel frightened. I tried hard to speak; it took a lot of effort to find my voice and for my mouth to form the words.

"Am I talking to you now?"

I could feel the energy of Melanie, Josh, Baz, and Poppy in the room, and as they replied, "Yes, we're here," I opened my eyes.

I felt shaky still as the DMT world dissipated and I could see them all. But, oh! Their faces! Coloured in pinks, greens, and blues, I could feel their concern and feel their smiles; their emotions were colours. I've learned since that pink represents love, blue is happiness, and friendship is green. I could see pinks and greens and blues in Josh, Melanie, and Robin. They all looked like beautiful ethereal elves made of woven fabric. Baz and Poppy were greens and blues (this made sense as they hadn't got the depth of love for me that showed pink on the faces of my family). Baz's hair was fascinating to me, like ribbons of embroidered cotton, and I reached to touch it.

The return to reality was rapid. Within five minutes, I was excitedly telling them as best I could about what I had experienced. Already, it was fading though, and although I struggled to verbalise what had happened to me, I felt euphoric for a while afterwards. Josh went next but coughed as the smoke irritated his throat so much. He experienced nothing other than discomfort. Melanie, however, had the most notable reaction. She couldn't relax, like when she had tried Salvia. There is something in Melanie that simply will not allow her to relinquish control, particularly in the company of large groups – regardless of how close the relationships are.

She began giggling and saying, "Wow… wow… WOW!"

Covering her face with her hands, in what seemed like embarrassment – her whole demeanour was animated and childlike.

"It's like, I don't know. I can't explain what I'm seeing." She continued laughing and looking occasionally at Robin.

"The colours are amazing; you all look like cartoons."

Poppy was writing down everything Melanie said so that she could read it later once she had come back from the trip.

"The patterns are amazing; I can't describe them. I can see everything you can see, but it's all gorgeous, like a kaleidoscope. The lampshades have butterfly wings, and the wallpaper looks like it's made of fabric!"

She interacted with us in a similar way to how I had, looking at hair and its texture, the colours of pinks and greens in our faces. What was surprising about Melanie's experience was how she could vocalise throughout exactly how she was feeling and her awareness of her situation, almost as if the DMT world was overlaying and existing alongside her earthly reality.

In the kitchen later, we were discussing our experiences when Melanie suddenly blurted out, "I want to do it again, now."

We all looked at her, surprised.

"I don't think it was right for me that time," she explained. "I was too aware of you lot looking at me and I felt stupid. I couldn't relax."

I understood what she meant. The giggling and hiding of her face showed her discomfort at her surroundings, which appeared to have affected her experience and her ability to let go.

"Can I do it again and you all stay in here except Baz and Poppy?"

"Yeah, okay." We nodded.

We were all happy to let her try, as we could see she was disappointed with her first go, but unlike Salvia, she had sensed there was something more to learn – something positive.

Baz, Melanie, and Poppy went back into the living room for another go. Robin, Josh, and I stood around in the kitchen like a set of lemons, quietly conferring about how the first session had gone. It transpired that Robin had no desire to try it at all, owing to a fear of psychedelics in general. I wondered if he had had an unpleasant experience in the past.

After around fifteen minutes, we heard movements. Baz and Poppy burst into the kitchen, sporting red-rimmed eyes and looking extremely emotional. We hardly had time to query what had happened before Melanie appeared, her face streaming with tears. We were very concerned for her and didn't know how to react until Melanie reached for Robin.

Clasping both his hands in hers, she smiled and laughed joyously through her tears.

"It's real. It's real, Robin!" she sobbed, throwing her arms around him. She couldn't contain her joy at whatever had happened to her.

"I curled up on my side on the sofa with just Baz and Poppy in the room. Poppy sat away to one side, ready to discreetly make notes of what would occur, while Baz gave me the medicine. I managed five pulls of the pipe, determined to breathe in as much as I could – more than last time. As soon as I felt the journey begin, I lay down and closed my eyes. I could feel the loud, high-pitched purring as the vibrations shuddered through my whole body. I could feel some mischievous energy or entity. It felt like it was teasing me, telling me it was more powerful than I was. I thought *Oh, I remember you from last time!* I decided I was going to let myself go and accept whatever fate awaited me."

"I think that's the key," Baz said and nodded. "I think Melanie has some kind of block that was stopping her from accepting the trip last time."

"Colours and patterns surrounded me," she continued. "I had no eyes or earthly body, but I could see with my consciousness. I was in them, and I *was* them. Fluttering, buzzing little entities buzzed around me, excited to welcome me. I could feel their individual identities. Scallop-edged in an ever-changing fluidity of colours, they were the collective consciousness of everyone who had ever lived, both on earth and before, and I just knew I was one of them. I was with the source of my own and all creation. I tried to communicate, but it was impossible, as I was still human. I recognised them, and I told them telepathically how much I'd missed them and loved them so, so much. They loved and had missed me too; I just knew that. I giggled with childlike love and joy. I felt so innocent and pure and with colours dancing and bursting around me, I told them, 'Thank you! Thank you!'"

We all listened intently and smiled at her exhilaration and joy. Melanie was relating something we could only begin to try to imagine.

"Into my vision came another fluttering entity, and I immediately recognised it as my baby. The soul that never existed on earth was here with me. I cocooned it in my consciousness and love, and we floated together as one. I could feel the maternal energy in me holding close and telling my baby how I missed it, and it wrapped me in reassurance

157

and love." (A few years previously, Melanie had suffered a miscarriage, so what she was relaying to us blew our minds!)

Turning to Baz and Poppy, she explained, "I physically opened my eyes and was aware of you two in the room, so I closed them again and the entities were still there. I said out loud, 'They're letting me stay', and to the collective consciousness I said telepathically, *I'm so grateful*. I didn't know how to convey my thanks to them. I felt my experience and visit must end soon, so I said aloud to Baz and Poppy, 'Would you mind leaving the room so that I can be alone with them (the collective consciousness entities)?' I heard you both leaving the room and I was alone with the entities. I used my mind to tell them, *I love you so much, I want to stay with you, I don't want to be without you again*. They were so loving and told me they would always be there, waiting for me, were part of me, and would always love me.

"At that point, I knew that if I stayed with them, I would never be my human, earthly self again. I would never see my human family again, and they loved and needed me. The entities began to dance for me – a kind of farewell display of blooming colours and beautiful yellow and black geometric patterns. They showed me I could be brave and strong, and I left with this wonderful experience and lesson they had bestowed upon me. I felt so lucky!

"It was time to leave, so with great concentration, I focused on my mind's eye and deliberately slowed the colours and movements until they became blurred greys and browns, like clouds underwater. I opened my eyes. Tears were still running down my cheeks, and the energy and spirituality in the room were tangible. I stood up and came to find you all."

We all stood rooted to the spot, speechless and very emotional for a moment. Melanie had told us something we had no understanding of. She was exhausted, but the euphoria was visible in her for a good while after. The rest of the evening was spent in quiet contemplation of what we had experienced. We put on some calming music until we all felt sleepy and went to bed with our inner thoughts.

Since then, I have had a similar experience with DMT to the one Melanie had, commonly known as a 'breakthrough'. This means travelling the journey of patterns and other entities and breaking through to the collective consciousness. I concluded after my own experience that the setting of love and comfort, and trusting that the people around you are truly focused on your well-being, is imperative. Trust, love, and connection are necessary for the propulsion you need to get to 'the other side'.

Is what we experienced 'real'? Having visited the so-called collective consciousness, I and millions of others believe so. An equal number say it's hallucinations. I'm not here to debate it one way or another. I do feel that on my last day on earth, the moment that my human life ends, the vibrations will take me home. I am spending time now reading up on NDEs (near-death experiences). From what I have learned so far, coupled with my discoveries, I believe and hope that science and spirituality can work together to investigate DMT in the human body. I guess I'm searching for comfort and confirmation that my consciousness will go on after death. This has become important to me, especially now I'm over sixty. Like Mandy, DMT showed me another way, and for that, I am eternally grateful.

Our DMT foray intrigued my other daughter, Charlotte. One Saturday after our weekly yoga class, we were having our usual cuppa in the Co-op Café, and she told me she wanted to attend an Ayahuasca ceremony. Her desire did not surprise me, but she wanted to leapfrog over other psychedelics and into a potential twelve hours of an unknown assault on her psyche.

She told me, "I've read about it a lot and I want to do it."

I admit I tried to convince her to try DMT or mushrooms first as a shorter and less intense experience, but who was I to say? I was no expert.

"You know, Mum, it's not like I've never done drugs before," she said, rolling her eyes at me in derision.

I tried to explain a little better, bringing finances and availability into the mix.

"It's up to you. I get why you want to try Ayahuasca, but unless you've got a few thousand in your holiday fund, it isn't going to happen any time soon. Plus, what if you got there and hated it? Then you're stuck for twelve hours wrestling with spirit panthers and puking demons into a plastic bucket."

I seemed to be making some headway, so I went in with the clincher,

"We've already got some DMT made. We can do it together and then you'll know for definite if Ayahuasca is something you want to do."

Notoriously reluctant to concede a point, Charlotte huffed a little more before agreeing it sounded like a reasonable compromise. We decided we would host Charlotte's DMT experience at her own house. The kids were away so we wouldn't be disturbed, and she would feel comfortable in her home environment.

Charlotte chose to have some subtle meditation music when she inhaled from the pipe, and we all sat quietly while she took four pulls. Lying back, she appeared very happy, smiley, and not at all nervous. After a minute or so, her body visibly relaxed. For the next ten minutes, she and Josh, her hubby Adz and I were quiet, but when she opened her eyes, she was euphoric and animatedly chatty.

"I was in the parade! Music and figures were dancing with me, like this," she exclaimed, waving her arms about.

"It was like being carried along in a parade of music and colours. When I opened my eyes, the room and you lot were cartoons!"

She was thrilled at whatever she'd seen and wanted to do it again. Josh filled the pipe, but on her first pull, she began to cough, her eyes streaming. "It's burnt; I can't breathe it in." She grimaced. "No, it's not right."

We abandoned the second attempt. Either the DMT was burned the second time, or it was warning us not to be greedy and impatient! Like any drug, DMT demands respect and a bit of practice, especially if you've never smoked. Later, and after a few similar experiences, we changed to using a tiny water bong that filters the smoke and removes the harshness.

Charlotte and Adz had both dabbled in recreational drugs way before I ever knew about it. Charlotte and Melanie had gone to a rave in some woodland a few years prior and had enjoyed going to occasional electronic music events together. As is often the case with siblings, their relationship had recently soured, so these days they had only been in touch at special family events. At Easter, there was a slight but important shift. Melanie had organised an Easter egg hunt for Louis and the rest of the family, and she invited their dad, Adrian, Charlotte and Adz, and their children, Ethan and Peter. It was a beautiful, sunny day. Josh and I were surprised but pleased to find them all chattering away when we arrived. Melanie and Robin had snacks and drinks out on the table under their enormous gazebo. I envied their garden, which Robin had worked on all summer. Complete with a fishpond, stunning flowers, plants, and lovely rattan garden furniture, it was the perfect space for peaceful gatherings.

The Easter egg hunt was fun, with the children running about and playing noisily. The afternoon passed easily with talking, eating and relaxation until eventually the kids quietened and dusk fell.

"Why don't you see if Adz's mum can have the kids tonight? You could stay over," Melanie suggested to Charlotte. Turning to me, she said, "We can all have a good evening and a few drinks if you fancy it?"

Adrian was happy to stay a while longer, but he had always been more comfortable in his own bed, so said he'd not stay the night. A lot of "Are you sures", were bandied about, but we all agreed we'd like that very much. I was quietly delighted. This was progress for Melanie and Charlotte, and I was proud of Melanie for making the move.

With the little ones delivered and drinking hot chocolate at their paternal grandparents' house, we settled into the evening. It wasn't long before Happy-Chappy Robin suggested Mandy join us. Charlotte and Adz hadn't touched Mandy since they became parents, and both were very reticent about any now, but this wasn't a problem. Josh, Melanie, Robin, and I had one pill each and settled into quiet music and easy conversations under the night sky. I could see Charlotte enviably eyeing my little tin, which contained another couple of pills.

"Just have half if you like," I offered. She considered for a moment before accepting, asking Adz, "Do you want the other half?" Adz, always the more cautious of the couple, declined. He was happy enough with a full bottle of whiskey he'd brought from home when he dropped the kids off at their granny's. I snapped a pill in half and Charlotte washed it down with water. What a beautiful evening for connection and good company. We looked up at the moon and stars above us. The only sounds were the tap of glasses on the table and the murmur of our conversation. Suddenly, the gazebo's steps creaked, and we all froze.

"Hiya!" It was my granddaughter Kelly just popping home for whatever teenagers pop home suddenly for. "What are you guys up to?" We all were like rabbits in the headlights, eyes round and shining like a gaggle of nocturnal bush babies and looking way too happy for sitting in a back garden gazebo.

"Hi!!!!!" we all chorused too loudly, grinning with varying degrees of manic enthusiasm.

"Where are you off tonight?" Melanie asked, in her best maternal and dependable adult voice. "Is Daniel picking you up?" Daniel was Kelly's boyfriend and he had a car. Melanie was trying to gauge how long we had before Kelly figured out all was not as it seemed. Too late – Kelly dragged up a chair and sat down for a natter. It is either a tribute to Melanie's parenting skills or, more likely, Kelly's acting skills and tact, that at nineteen she gave no sign whatsoever that she knew her parents, grandparents, aunt, and uncle were well and truly off their tits.

Eventually, Kelly left for a more responsible night out, and with a collective sigh of relief at getting away with it, we returned to our socialising. Charlotte was by now snuggled up in a blanket and happily waxing lyrical about the stars and life in general. Adz was knocking back whiskey after whiskey shot and lying with his eyes closed, just enjoying listening to the surrounding conversation. Charlotte had asked him a few times if he wanted to change his mind about the half pill, but he said he'd feel better with a few drinks instead. It felt good having the family together, talking easily and just enjoying being with each other – no drama or mistrust.

I'm not sure at what point DMT was mentioned and discussed, but Adrian decided the time was right, as he'd had no Mandy and very little to drink. We all agreed it would be a suitable moment for him as it was only family gathered around. Josh prepared the pipe, and we all fell silent. Adrian sat back and, although very nervous, took three pulls, then closed his eyes. There was absolute quiet as we all bowed our heads and respected his journey. He spoke quietly, with lots of "wow!" and "amazing!" which is common for anyone experiencing the sudden rush of colour and patterns. I glanced upwards and could see Melanie smiling slightly as she recognised and empathised with the feelings her father was having in the world he now inhabited.

Adrian came round quickly and despite us asking about his experience, he seemed either unable or unwilling to expand on anything other than that he saw patterns and colours. I understood it. Often you need to take time to process the experience and six smiling and curious people pressing you to talk about it isn't helpful, regardless of how well-meaning they may be.

The temperatures had dropped colder, and we snuggled up in the blankets brought out by Robin. Charlotte cuddled up close to me, and I kissed her forehead, telling her I loved her. I looked around at our little group, their faces now illuminated by candles, and I knew the time was right. Here were the people closest to me. The ones who knew me better than I knew myself, the ones I'd shared my heart with.

"I want to do DMT too," I told them. "I know I've had a little Mandy, but it feels right. I feel open to it tonight."

I asked Josh to fill the pipe and Melanie came to sit next to me. Melanie is the one who keeps everyone quiet and respectful of each experience, and I trusted her to encourage me to take the extra pull I needed to travel as far as I needed to go.

"Wrap yourself up, Mum, and when you feel you want to close your eyes, curl up and get comfy."

I nodded.

"When you think you've had enough, I'll give you another, okay?"

I nodded again.

"Yes, okay."

She passed me the pipe. It's so strange that the first time I had DMT, I could recall exactly how many pulls of the pipe I'd had, and how the sounds and colours had hurled me into another realm. Not this time. I vaguely heard Melanie, from what seemed like far, far away, encouraging me to take "one more". Then I left this world.

Everyone, the garden, the night sky, everything just fell away, and I was in a cloud of orange and yellow luminous space. My consciousness moved slowly and fluidly as part of the matter, which felt warm, like gazing into the sun on a hot beach. I slowly sank, turning and snuggling into the blanket, but from the warmth of the orange clouds came hundreds of small floating and sparkling creatures. I say creatures, maybe just beings. They had no form but sparkled and approached me excitedly, some zipping around above me but most sinking to envelop me with their love. There is no other word in our language. Why is it so frustratingly restricted? Love wasn't even half a description of the feeling. It covered me. It held me within it. I absorbed it and felt I *was* love. I felt safe, like I never wanted to leave. If this was forever, I wanted to stay.

It seemed like an eternity, yet only minutes had passed before I could feel a lift. The entities were rising from my body, from whatever form I had taken, and were floating up and up, laughing and dancing as they rose. "Come back!" my consciousness called. "Come back. Don't go."

I could feel grief and panic and abandonment, but they seemed happy to be leaving me.

"Take me with you," I pleaded, looking desperately into the orange light as they faded.

Then, for the slightest of moments, they all reappeared.

"You *can* come back. We are always here; we will always be here and so will you."

Then they were gone, and I opened my eyes. Even now, the recounting of this fills me with deeply embedded emotion.

The others say I turned and reached toward the sky, but I have no recollection of moving at all. Like Adrian, I couldn't process what had happened. I didn't want to talk about it, and I attempted to get back to conversing about simpler things and enjoying the evening, but it was there, on my mind all night. It has been on my mind periodically ever since.

After that, Adrian said his goodbyes and left while we just snuggled and talked deep into the night. Adz finished his whiskey, and one by one we all agreed it was time for bed. Josh and I were also tired, so with lots of hugs and kisses, we left, too.

The next morning, we called Charlotte to see how the sleepover had been. Hooting with laughter, she informed us that poor Adz, too nervous to take the other half of the pill, had spent the hour after we left vomiting up the bottle of whiskey he'd consumed, whereas everyone else had risen bright, perky, and ready for a good breakfast. Looking back, I don't think the evening alone was enough to repair Charlotte and Melanie's relationship, but there was a mutual trust in sharing the night that may contribute as the building blocks for the future. They have stayed in touch and talk occasionally. They even went to a gig together not long ago, so maybe Mandy is still doing her work there.

Adz may reconsider the Mandy/alcohol dilemma and I, well, I *believe*. I believe DMT has a lot more to show me, that you shouldn't jump the queue past the patterns and colours corridor. It seems disrespectful, and I need to travel it in its entirety. Was one pill of Mandy the opening to the breakthrough? I believe it's possible. MDMA channels love and together with DMT, they allowed me to see it all. I believe absolutely that another realm exists alongside this and that it is waiting for us all to return.

Melanie, Robin, Josh, and I hosted a small DMT ceremony some months later for a friend of Melanie's whom we had never met before. Simon was in his mid-thirties, stocky and well-muscled. He was generous with his easy smile and engaging manner. He was a live wire and arrived laden down with a twelve-pack of cider as a gesture of thanks. This was very kind of him, but unnecessary. We were holding a ceremony to share the love and lessons DMT honoured us with, not in return for money or other offerings.

We liked Simon from the start. There was no room for awkward silences, as he simply did not stop talking. He was well-travelled and had tragically lost his sister in a road accident a few years before. We wanted to help him process this and let DMT show him that hope and the spirit lives on. We all looked on open-mouthed as he related his full life story to date without pausing for breath. His smiles and intermittent wild gesticulations left us exhausted by his enthusiasm. With a few stuttering attempts, Robin eventually broke the flow.

"Right, mate," he said. "So how come you wanted to do DMT?"

"Well, this is it, see! I've recently been diagnosed with ADHD (attention deficit hyperactivity disorder)."

No kidding! He explained he had felt for a long time that there was 'something else' he needed to find. Cliché as it sounds, he was one of the many of us that seems to reach a stage where we are looking for something we can't explain. Maybe the need he felt was in connection with his sister, maybe not. We had every confidence that DMT would show him whatever it was he needed to know.

Although Simon was excited and ready to try DMT, his ADHD made it difficult for him to trust us with the process. He insisted on holding the pipe himself, which for a beginner wasn't the best idea. The initial rush of the drug and bodily vibrations could have caused him to drop it. Hot pipes on the skin and surrounding furniture aren't the ideal scenario for a relaxed experience. He took the pulls well, however, and lay back with his eyes closed. For the first time in over an hour and a half, he fell silent.

Simon never really told us what his experience was like, other than he saw a female figure playfully beckoning him to follow her into a lake. He described her as flirtatious and mischievous, and of course, came the usual exclamations of "Wow!" and "Amazing!" Immediately after DMT is way too soon to even try to process what has happened in its entirety.

He did tell us though that he wanted to try again, and he went home with an open-ended invitation that we would be happy to see him again, if, and when, he felt ready. Josh and I reflected on the evening's events after Simon had left. We both sensed that at times, he appeared to be confused and distracted. Like Melanie, he was unable to let go fully. Bearing in mind he didn't know Josh and me very well, this was unsurprising. His ADHD also doubtless had an effect psychologically, in that when DMT sent the female entity to tempt him to go further, he was unable to follow her to the next realm, even though he knew it was waiting. I also knew that feeling well, and it was what pushed me forward with recreational drug experimentation after Mandy. The ever-present issue hanging over my friendships was being slowly addressed, but the 'something else', has hovered and niggled me throughout my life as a faint shadow, passing in my peripheral thoughts now and then.

My life was just fine as it was. Josh and I had a lovely home. My relationship with my children was a constant source of happiness to me, and my business, although stressful at times, was something I was proud of. So, what was this 'something else' we all seek? It has taken me a long, long time to conclude that it is, for me, a calm mind. It's that simple. Josh and I have met so many people since being introduced to Mandy, and most, especially the women, would happily and without any doubt label themselves as 'spiritual' to some level. Most, when pressed, would add that they were enlightened, liberated, and part of a tribe (you know, the one your 'vibe' attracts). They live on the edges of a true hippie lifestyle but have ordinary jobs and pay the bills like the rest of us. Some will go on retreats, spend weekends camping with other like-minded folks, and attend music festivals and raves. Many complete the image by buying ethnic clothing and decking out their bohemian-style homes with strings of jingly elephants and wall hangings. They are sometimes vegan and have alternative ideas from the masses. And right down deep inside, but up there too, is an almost tangible aura, the Something Else, which is the search for peace and a calm mind. Mostly, they are ordinary people like you and me.

It was at a camp-out that I realised what a lack of respect for DMT looks like, and it's not something I would ever repeat. It was late the next summer that a group of friends, including Ally, Melanie, and Robin, all met at a local campsite for probably the last outdoor gathering before winter. There was a mixture of people there, all like-minded, friendly people who, as the day turned into night, took their drug of choice. It appeared to split down the middle into those snorting lines of cocaine and those happily tipping back pills. The air around us was fragrant with the smoke from numerous joints of weed.

We were chatting with one guy who had expressed to Josh by private Facebook messages that he'd like to experience DMT. Josh, being the kind and generous guy he is, offered to bring some along so that he could sit in the guy's van away from the others and be his 'trip-sitter', making sure he was okay, and that his experience was a safe one. As it happened, the guy had drunk so much alcohol, smoked so much weed, and taken so much Mandy, that he had wisely decided it wasn't the right time for him. Others, however, had different ideas. Somehow, it got around that we had DMT with us. Several of us were huddled on the bed in Melanie and Robin's van. We were all getting sleepy and were coming down from what we had taken earlier. Most of the others had topped up their MDMA by dabbing a fingertip into the small, plastic bag of yellow-tinged crystals and putting it on their tongues, as you would a bag of sherbet. The odd one or two people had sniffed the occasional line of MDMA and were stupefied with lack of sleep and whatever drugs other they'd taken.

Melanie suddenly shouted out, "Josh, can Ally try DMT?"

There was a mumbled agreement of "Yeah, can we too?" from the others. We weren't happy about the way this was going, as we were shattered and ready for bed, and a DMT trip should be in a calm, quiet environment. Melanie knew from her own experience that a cramped campervan full of drugged-up, half-asleep people was not the ideal scenario to take DMT or to have a positive experience, so it surprised me she was suggesting it.

"No, Melanie," I said. "It's too cramped and everyone has had too much to drink or taken too many drugs. Anyway, it's late; I'm ready to go to sleep."

She wasn't giving up.

"Go on," she appealed to Josh instead. "It's not that late. These guys may not get the chance to do it any other time."

I tried again.

"Look, we should have done it right at the beginning of the night. It's too late now and it'll mean getting everything out of the van and we're ready for bed. It may not work anyway with all the other stuff they've had," I reasoned, gesturing mainly to Ally, who appeared to have already nodded off. "Let's do it another time."

I'd love to say Josh and I won the argument, but no. All four DMT virgins in the van had a measured dose of DMT. By the time we'd given the last one, we were asleep on our feet. We were exhausted and just wanted the night to end. I was right too about the effects of alcohol and mixing drugs on the DMT trip.

Never have we seen such a bizarre collection of responses. One girl was thrashing about so much that we had to hold her limbs still as she laughed and talked to African-looking people in a blue jungle. Ally murmured and muttered to a male entity whilst attempting to masturbate. Shocked, we threw a blanket over her at that point and to date have never told her the truth about what she did. We know she would be mortified. Another of the guys, so stoned he couldn't open his eyes to see or hold the pipe, took five strong pulls and fell into a deep and snoring sleep from which he refused to wake up to any kind of lucidity. He staggered blindly to his tent much later, supported by his girlfriend. Melanie had attempted to stop anyone coming into the van (Robin in particular, who had been left outside with the coke snorters) and disturbing the trippers, but the whole event simply wasn't under the right circumstances and had become farcical.

Apart from the guy who had fallen asleep, everyone had their own stories of the event, which within minutes they forgot. At 6 a.m., Josh and I went back to our camper to get some sleep, but despite our tiredness, it didn't come easy. I felt we'd betrayed DMT somehow by allowing it to be used as party entertainment. I was unhappy that we'd given in to pressure against our better judgment and upset that those involved had not had an authentic experience. They would doubtless now never want to try DMT again because the experience won't have seemed like much of a big deal. Before falling into an uneasy sleep that night, Josh and I both agreed never again to abuse DMT and disrespect the realms we were invited to visit. We will now extract fresh batches for acquaintances to experience in our home as a gift. They will be quiet affairs, such as befits the strongest, most welcoming, and hospitable plant medicine (although some may call it a drug) available to man. In retrospect, it was a lesson well learned.

Josh and I began making our own DMT because after researching a lot, we were interested in the spiritual aspect and wanted to be more self-reliant. We have tried other recreational drugs simply out of curiosity and almost without exception, only once, we never take anything else with any regularity other than Mandy. In absolute honesty, both Josh and I agree that nothing has ever given us the feelings of connection and love we have in Mandy, and after all, that's what we were yearning for. We have made only four batches of DMT in two years. It isn't a party drug, in our opinion – more of an irregular 'calling' when you feel the time is right. We now occasionally smoke DMT with a tiny water bong out in nature (we once did it sitting in Sherwood Forest on the edges of a holiday camp). I never smoke now to have a 'breakthrough', only to sit and look, really look at the beauty of the trees and plants around us. It's as if for ten wonderful minutes the world has been overlaid with a 'beautifying' filter and my eyes have been fully opened. Trees show us their life and their inner spirit. Each blade of grass stands out in relief against a carpet of emeralds. I truly feel that in everyday life, our vision of nature has been dumbed down just so that our senses aren't overwhelmed by our environment. The teachings of DMT are again ones of connection, this time with nature. These lessons keep reminding me to have hope, to appreciate what I sometimes take for granted and to look beyond the ordinary, to look for the beauty and purpose in every living thing. Even earwigs!

RAVES

To my innocent mind, my kids used to go to discos. Now, though, I knew they had been returning pop-eyed and off their heads on recreational drugs. They had been taking ecstasy pills, and they had been going to raves. Back in the day, Carl had sporadic bouts of worrying swellings on his face and sometimes on one foot or one arm. It was a bizarre affliction and was an issue throughout his teenage years. His face and occasionally a limb, hand or foot, would swell alarmingly, then revert to normal a day later. The doctor couldn't find anything wrong and put it down to some allergy. There followed years of trial and error, attempting to find the cause. I changed washing powder, softener, shampoo, and food. *Was it the dog?* We tried everything without success. Eventually, it became just something Carl tolerated. He wasn't in pain, so he just went to bed until his face went back to normal. Poor Carl earned the nickname 'Hamster Face' and when the swelling was at its worst, he also had 'Hamster Feet!'

Melanie once told me a tale about her returning from town and coming into the garden gate. Unbeknownst to her, Carl had sneaked downstairs to watch TV while the house was empty.

He looked like The Elephant Man, lurching and thumping around the living room on one enormous foot. Melanie caught a glimpse of him just as Carl's best mate, Faz, turned up to see if Carl fancied going out. Melanie valiantly attempted to convince him that Carl wasn't in. Curious about the noise outside, Carl pulled back the curtain and looked out of the window. Faz stared back, both fascinated and appalled in equal measure.

"Errrrrm, who's that in your house, Mel?"

The facial disfigurements of a bulging forehead, swollen shut eyes, and massive rubber lip bobbing around on his chin had rendered Carl unrecognisable, even to his best friend. Thank goodness that after a few years, the swellings gradually lessened, and then disappeared completely. The puzzle of Hamster Face lay dormant for over twenty years.

After we got home from a recent camp with Mandy, I was looking through photos of the event. Josh and I agreed that we all looked very glowing, but weirdly, some of our friends looked puffy, with heavily lidded eyes. We carried on looking through the pictures and, boom! Just like that, I smelled not only the coffee but the sweet scent of absolute certainty. Carl had been on drugs! I thought back to all those years ago. Yeah, it was generally weekends. I would work evenings and I'd see him in the morning fumbling in the kitchen with sausage fingers and seeing with only one eye. I phoned him.

"Carl, you know when you used to get Hamster Face?" I didn't get any further. He began to laugh loudly, then proceeded to tell me something quite shocking. Carl has never been able to take tablets, not even aspirin, as he can't swallow them. Because of this, he became infamous at raves for being able to chew dry pills (no mean feat, as they are vile to the taste). He told me that people would come and give him a pill just to watch him chew and swallow it dry, and therefore he got his drugs both free and in large quantities. I asked him if it was Mandy he took and it horrified me when he admitted he had no idea because after a while he just chewed anything he was given, in any amount. The swelling and allergy had originated from the enormous cocktail of random pills he was taking. I can't believe he got away with it so lightly, considering.

As a parent, I know how easy it is to miss signs of drug use. Solvent abuse was causing concern in the mid-eighties, and glue-sniffing was the most common form among teenagers. Spraying aerosols into a paper bag, and then inhaling the captured fumes caused nausea, discoordination, and slurred speech, among other effects. This was a habit prevalent among young people and many parents simply closed their eyes to the possibility that their child could be at risk, although we all were aware of it. Interestingly, solvent abuse is not illegal.

In 1986, there was a campaign by the popular children's TV programme, *Grange Hill*, to raise awareness about drugs in general. The tag line was 'Just Say No', and it was well promoted by the media. One of the main characters was a schoolboy, Zammo. It showed him having taken an overdose of heroin. Watching the show with Melanie, who was only seven, I was reminded of a girl in my high school who died of an overdose in London. However, a schoolboy in an unknown London borough, on a children's television programme, just wasn't relatable to me. Others who watched the programme had a similar view. We knew it was about drugs, but in our small village, heroin was a faraway and almost fictional threat. In contrast, there was no warning programme about recreational drug use. Cannabis, speed, and various other drugs were in widespread distribution, but no one mentioned them, and Mandy, the 'love drug', had just begun to appear on the scene.

The reason we and many others take Mandy is still for the feeling of affinity with others as a party drug, rather than the therapeutic medicine I believe they should approve it for. Users come together to dance and have fun – and that's fine, but people must be careful. During the COVID pandemic, there was a post doing the rounds on social media aimed at the anti-vaxxers, showing a group of people at a rave, the accompanying text being, *You won't have the vaccine but will jump on a dropped bag of pills faster than a seagull on chips.* Whilst I make no statement of opinion about vaccines, I know this post to be spot on. I've seen individuals scanning the floor at the end of a rave for dropped bags of drugs with no idea what they might contain if they find one.

A rave to me meant hundreds of sweating bodies in a variety of colourful outfits, dancing and waving their arms about to wordless, pounding, rhythmic beats. I'd seen the film, *Kevin and Perry Go Large* loads of times, so I was an expert, right? Ha! well I was kind of right, and it was only a matter of time before Mandy showed us its fun and mischievous side. One of the largest and most well-known raves was advertised in Leeds. A nod to the old Acid House warehouse parties, it promised to be an amazing night. A group of ten of us decided to go there together – safety in numbers and all that. We excitedly bought tickets for our very first rave.

Josh and I spent months searching for and discarding various outfits and worrying about whether another COVID lockdown would see the rave cancelled at the last minute. We felt nervous but excited in equal amounts. I decided on a psychedelic patterned bell-sleeved mini dress, yellow tights with multicoloured bubbles all over them, and a pair of specs shaped like palm trees. I looked like a lunatic. Melanie was wearing giant luminescent butterfly wings and Josh had on a t-shirt with a smiley face on the front and an over-shirt plastered in a neon print of reefers, mushrooms, and cartoon pills. I considered what I would say if we had another unexpected meeting with a police person. *Don't worry, Officer, nothing to see here; we're just off to the pub for one!*

The atmosphere in the queue to get in was a hum of anticipation. Hundreds of ravers, all with just one intention, to have fun and dance together. Once inside, the heat and sheer mass of bodies were overwhelming, and, nervously clutching our bottles of water, we had to push our way to a small space by one of the stages. I was the only person scared to retrieve my pills from my bra in the middle of the crowd. Each nervous glance seemed to confirm that everyone was watching me. I was paranoid about my impending crime and must have looked extremely suspicious. Conversely, a bemused Melanie knocked hers back in full view of everyone with the cavalier attitude of the accomplished raver. She then guided me to the already wet and stinking portaloos to take my first one. She stood outside holding the door shut while I swigged down my pill with some water and crept out through the piss and discarded toilet paper, expecting to feel the hand of the law on my shoulder at any second. I guess it takes some getting used to.

The rave was being held in an enormous old warehouse, which, apart from electricity, was completely abandoned. There were hundreds of people there, all noisy and eager to dance. It was a wonderful sight. Most were in colourful and crazy outfits like ours. What a night! So many people, all big-eyed on pills or MDMA. Music pounded from a variety of stage sets and lights beamed and flashed everywhere. Josh and I moved from room to room, taking in the sights, sounds, and varying states of high. Some ravers were dancing and yelling in conversation with each other over the music. Others were slumped, seemingly unseeing, on benches while the event just happened around them. I felt great. I ended up dancing on a table waving glow sticks (kindly supplied by the organisers). Josh and I shared another ecstasy pill around an hour after our first, but found we got tired way sooner than on our camps, where we rarely started to flag until four in the morning.

As the night wore on, we noticed that other drugs were readily available and being taken, including a lot of coke and speed.

We saw a few individuals stumbling around under the influence of ketamine. The event security who were monitoring things, were on the ball. At one point, I sat down for a rest, and a young guy began leaning heavily on me and anyone close to him. He looked semi-conscious; his eyes were rolling into the back of his head and he was sweating profusely. A security man came over and gave him a bottle of water, which is exactly what he needed. That situation was a real eye-opener.

By 1.30 a.m., we were all raved out and ready for our beds. I'm sure many will have stayed until the final kick-out, but upon trying and failing to get a taxi to pick us up at the venue, we walked into town to grab one at the office. Looking back, I missed the closeness and connection people had at our previous gatherings. The event's slogan was 'People Come Together', but neither I nor Josh felt that vibe at all. People didn't hug each other or strangers that much, and the music was far too loud to hold a decent conversation.

Melanie, an unlikely Cupid, dressed in her bedraggled butterfly wings, somehow managed to navigate the five rooms and the crowds to introduce Ally to a spectacular-looking guy. He was a Legolas from *Lord of the Rings* look-a-like, tall with long white-blond hair, and oozing charisma and sex appeal in equal parts. He was so beautiful that he appeared to glow in the dark. As we left, Ally and the elf were wrapped around each other in a potentially reproductive 'connection', so I guess the rave's tag line was apt for them at least.

Neither Josh nor I have been put off going to raves. I can't wait to attend a rave in the woods. These are basically what they say on the tin – a rave in some woods, or maybe an abandoned area of some sort. They are also illegal. The illegal aspect I find strangely appealing, as I've long harboured a bizarre dream to participate in a floppy protest. I'm not overly concerned as to the cause I'd be protesting about, but I can picture myself happily grinning at the camera as two policemen carry me from my squatting position on the ground, refusing to move. Yes, I could see it now – me swinging between them as they carried me, each one holding an arm and a leg, dragging me toward the back doors of the police van. I'd be on telly, surely. My family would be so proud. Seriously though, they would. We're all slightly bonkers and rebellious when the moment takes us.

There was one woodland rave not long after the Leeds one, but unfortunately, Josh and I were away and couldn't attend. Melanie and Robin went, though, clambering over stiles and barbed wire fences and getting chased by cows, who probably thought it was late feeding time. They arrived at an old tunnel that was already throbbing and alive with lights and music from the decks at one end. It looked like a promising night, and they took their pills and joined the others already on the come-up. Inevitably, an hour later, the police arrived after a tip-off from some residential houses on the horizon somewhere. The organisers hadn't considered that sound travels miles at night. Three officers with torches eventually arrived, red-faced, with grass-stained trousers, which were torn from the barbed wire fences, and boots liberally coated with cow muck. After traversing the terrain and getting lost a few times, they spotted the party. The police didn't seem sure how to deal with the situation, so after a brief discussion between themselves, they allowed the attendees one more hour of raving. Pretty kind of them, considering. Mind you, they could have been called out to a pub brawl, so they got off easily with over two hundred happy dancers!

Melanie laughed and said, "They were asking everyone, 'Where did you get your drugs?' It's not like they were going to get an answer, but if they had, I just know it would have been, 'Him there!' And everyone would have just pointed at one another."

Being the amenable souls that ravers are, they all packed up after an hour and the police helped carry the gear through the fields, over the stiles, past the by-now disinterested cows and bent barbed wire, and back to the vehicles on the road. It had lasted only a couple of hours, but still worth it.

Melanie sighed happily. "The paperwork back at the police station probably took way longer."

FINDING MY WAY

I'm not mad keen on London as I find it very crowded and fast-paced for a day out. However, the culture there appeals to my love of both history and animals, so when Josh and I went down there for a weekend, I headed straight for the Museum of Natural History. My favourite exhibition is the dinosaurs, prehistoric man, and evolution through the ages. If you've never been to the Natural History Museum, I can highly recommend it. You will need at least three or four hours, but can easily spend a full day there. It also has an impressive and reasonably priced café where you can get a light lunch.

After exploring the interactive dinosaur exhibit (which houses a full-size moving, roaring, and realistic-enough-to-scare-the-kids Tyrannosaurus Rex), we headed to the café for lunch. Do you know when some days luck seems to be on your side? Well, this day it was on Josh's. We got ourselves a table number and joined the queue with our trays. Shuffling down the line, we perused the plated sandwiches, and bottles of juice, past the hot stand where we both chose jacket potatoes with cheese and further on, to the cakes. Just as we reached it, a lady came out, sagging under the weight of the most enormous Red Velvet cake. It was filled with cream and appeared to glow in a halo of ruby magnificence. Josh is a big, cuddly guy and much of his happiness on a minor level is provided by food. I could almost feel him shiver with anticipation as she placed it carefully on a cake stand and returned to the counter. Josh and I both spotted the rookie error immediately. Instead of pre-portioning the cake like all the others on display, she had simply left a knife on the stand so people could cut their own. I glanced at the little price sign. £1.99 per slice. I almost felt sorry for the café as I watched Josh grab the knife before she came back and hover it over the virgin cake.

"Babe, don't get too mu—"

Down it came, slicing through a slab of moist sponge, chocolate flakes, and fresh cream, separating a portion the size of a house brick. The animation on Josh's face as he held out his £2 coin for a plate he could barely lift in one hand was a picture. You'd think he'd been awarded an MBE. I paid for my sandwich and a couple of drinks and then followed him to the table. As he happily munched his bargain booty, we chatted about the 'Evolution of Man' exhibit.

"So, humans were mixing plants and smoking them when the wheel was still a square," I mused as I ate my tuna on brown.

"They invented pipes and bongs basically before many other necessities of life. They were looking for enlightenment even then."

"It's the same with alcohol," added Josh, still chewing. "People judge drug use, yet what do they think alcohol is? Alcohol is yet again mixing plants to achieve an altered state of mind. It's been going on for centuries. Because it's legal and makes a lot of money for governments, it's seen as acceptable."

"And," I continued, "alcohol is the cause of more violent behaviour than is *ever* seen in recreational drug users. And it's readily available in any quantity legally!"

That got me considering how people currently attain their 'enlightenment' and relaxation. If it's cigarettes or alcohol, then we are already recreational drug users and possibly addicts. We just pay more tax on the legal stuff. Another question I asked myself is "How long can people go without their (cigarettes/alcohol) drug of choice?" I could go for three weeks, three months, or years without Mandy or DMT, but as a previous smoker, I know my limit then was around an hour before I craved a cigarette. It's currently a couple of hours before I need a coffee. When I thought about it that way, I became a little more baffled as to how the laws on drugs came into being, and how people happily using nicotine and alcohol would sneer at our relationship with Mandy. 'Judge not, lest ye be judged' as they say.

Cocaine, though, is different again! Remember that some of our camping friends were snorting lines of coke? I realised very quickly that it wasn't my thing at all. I tried my first (and last) line of coke at our very first drugs camp. By the time 2 a.m. arrived, the music was mellow, and everyone's buzz had plateaued. Mooching around and chatting to people, I noticed a few snorting lines of coke. Now I wasn't daft even then. I watch films and was quite aware of what it was, and I was curious. I sidled up to Robin.

"Robin, I know you aren't keen on it, but do you reckon one line of coke would be harmful? I've never tried it and I'm just curious as to what it's like."

Robin frowned slightly as he considered my request.

"It's not that great," he warned. "I get why you want to try it and it's not addictive just once, but are you sure? It's not like Mandy y'know,"

I assured him I wasn't going to be making a habit of it, but wanted to try it just once. Then at least I'd be able to make an informed judgement about it whilst satisfying my curiosity as to why people used cocaine. Was it another 'connection' drug?

"Right, stay there," he instructed, and disappeared into a group of camper vans. I stayed put.

A moment later he was back, happily flapping about in his poncho.

"Hey up, Ma-in-law!"

He flopped down next to me and glanced furtively around.

Like a stage magician whipping out a white rabbit, he produced his baccy tin, complete with a line already set up and a straw.

"Go on," he whispered. "That'll be enough to get you going, but don't tell Melanie."

I can't imagine I'd stopped, never mind wanted to get going again, but in for a penny and all that. I lined up the straw and sniffed up like I'd seen in movies, holding one nostril closed with a finger. I thought I must look like a right drugs pundit.

"For Christ's sake!"

It felt like I'd snorted wholegrain mustard or hot sauce.

"God, that's nasty!"

I tried to sniff downwards to get rid of the stuff. The back of my throat tasted chemical and bitter. Robin just grinned.

"Told ya! Just don't tell Melanie I gave it to you; she'll go mad if she knows I'm giving her mum coke."

I felt in absolutely no danger of keeping secrets from Melanie, as like a goldfish, Robin on drugs has a three-second memory. As Melanie came sauntering over, he leapt up to meet her.

"Babe! Babe! I've just given your mum her first line of coke."

I rolled my eyes, shook my head at him, and chuckled to myself. The coke did nothing for me at all, other than to taste revolting and burn my nostrils.

I don't like the effects of coke from what I've witnessed, either. On camps or any other get-togethers, the people on coke become angsty and paranoid, quick to be confrontational. Others just do not know what they're doing, especially if the user has also had a belly full of alcohol, like the naked lady we encountered later that year.

Now then, settle back, for what follows is a true and cautionary tale… It was winter. Picture the scene: a cold, dark night in December, around 9.30 p.m. There was a sprinkling of snow, and it was ball-shrivellingly freezing outside. Josh and I were snuggled up with our dog Rory on the sofa, watching a crime drama on Netflix, when the doorbell rang. Useless guard dog Rory and I pretended we hadn't heard it. It was way too cold out there to move from our comfy spot.

"Humph," grumbled Josh, getting up. "I bet it's a takeaway place with the wrong address."

Nodding in agreement, I carried on watching the telly. Minutes passed and Josh didn't come back. Suddenly, a strangled shout from outside pierced the silence.

"Helen!!! Come here quick!"

I got up quickly and peered through the window into the dark. The porch light was on, and I could just make out two figures on the steps. I left Rory snoozing on the sofa and hurried outside, worried that there was trouble over something. What confronted me beggared belief.

"Babe, come and help!"

Josh was in a right panic, and I wasn't surprised. Sliding down the steps, half on her naked backside, one hand hanging onto the frozen fence, was a young woman. She was a very attractive young woman, dressed (and I use the term loosely) in nothing but a scrap of lace. The bottom half was a thong that disappeared into her ample bum cheeks with barely half an inch of a landing strip in front. I couldn't help but stare, open-mouthed.

"Who's she? Where's she come from?" I stammered, looking up and down the dark empty road, my frozen breath misting the air.

"I've no idea," blabbered Josh, glancing around nervously. "What if it's a diversion to rob us?" (He plays way too many computer games.)

Attempting to engage the frightened-looking woman, I inched closer to her and spoke in a gentle tone, so as not to startle her further.

"Hiya, love, are you alright?" I'm a genius, me. Of course, she wasn't alright, it was minus one and she was wandering into strangers' gardens in the niff!

I worried she might be in danger of falling backwards into Josh, whose hands were hovering cautiously under her bare behind, just in case. I looked over her shoulder at him and whispered, "What do we do? We'll have to take her in."

At that moment, Naked Lady lost her footing again and lurched on cold, red stilettoed feet into my arms, nearly taking out my eyes with her equally frozen nipples as she did so. I didn't know what else to do but hug her.

"It's alright," I murmured as if to a lost puppy. Up close, I could see her pupils were black and enormous. "Have you taken ecstasy?"

I felt secretly pleased I knew enough to recognise the signs. She wobbled around in my arms, smiling seductively.

"No," she teased, whispering closely and warmly into my ear. "But I've had a LOT of coke!"

Oh, boy. By this point, Josh was on his mobile to poor Andy next door as she added that she was looking for her boyfriend, who knew him. She'd left her house looking for him after he'd gone to collect a takeaway, but in her confusion, she had arrived as a frozen dessert at the wrong door. I asked her where she lived, and she waved vaguely in the general direction of 'down the hill'. Andy confirmed from the pub that she lived a few doors away and he'd call her boyfriend to come to get her. I'm surprised poor Andy hasn't blocked our number by now.

Wrapping my cardigan around her shoulders, Josh and I delivered the poor lass back home.

"Come in!" She smiled, gesturing us inside, still wobbling around and falling against the door frame.

We were loath to leave her alone in the house in case she wandered off again and ended up either frozen to death in the wood opposite or picked up by some 'helpful' stranger, only to appear as a missing persons appeal on Crime Watch some months later. The dubious and potentially dangerous situation of being found in a naked, drugged-up woman's house, however, prompted us to stand guard, shivering, from the bottom of the steps until her boyfriend arrived. The poor fella screeched up in his car a few moments later. Chinese takeaway bag swinging wildly, he ran, red-faced up the steps, muttering, "Thanks, sorry," as he went.

A couple of days later, Andy popped around to see us.

"She's always doing stuff like that. It's awful for her boyfriend, and dangerous too! If anything had happened . . .!"

We nodded in agreement.

"Her boyfriend, Martin, is a mate of mine, and he's sick and tired of it."

I'm surprised Andy wasn't sick and tired of *us* and the bizarre happenings at our house since he'd moved in. First the van in his pit, and now this!

As soon as we closed the door, Josh started scrolling on his phone like a private detective. He had Andy on Facebook and was looking through his friends list.

"Martin, Martin, *aah*, here he is."

Josh clicked on his profile and there he was with his partner, Jessica. She looked a lot different. Smartly dressed, with impeccable makeup, and smiling innocently into the camera, she looked smart and classy. Josh clicked on her profile.

"Oh wow, look at this!"

Jessica's profile proudly stated that she was a teacher at the local primary school up the road. And herein lies the warning: Had we been different people, we could have ruined her future, and her life. Her full naked wander was captured clearly on our security camera for us to show or send to anyone. She could have died of cold in the woods across the road or been murdered. Worst-case scenarios, yes, but not impossible. Fortunately, she stumbled toward our door. Let's just say, however, that even if she runs out of sugar, you can bet your last Rolo that we will be the *last* people she comes to borrow any from. We learned there and then, not to do too many drugs and not to do them alone.

Like many people, my search for whatever I'm looking for has been via yoga, exercise, and music, among other things. Buying dangling elephants and bells and dressing in quirky clothing convinced me I must be on the right track. It took Josh searching for a takeaway meal, however, to confirm that peace of mind is what I craved. Mandy had introduced the connections; now I needed to be kinder to myself.

Worn out and burned out with work and the ups and downs of the COVID situation, we were desperate to get away, kick back and relax, just the two of us. The past year had been a wonderful, crazy time of discovery and personal joy, but we needed some 'us' time. Josh went online and put the metaphorical 'pin in the map', booking a night in an Airbnb in a small coastal village a hundred or so miles away. There wasn't much there, but the small shopping centre with original cobbled streets and traditional pubs was exactly what we needed. Unfortunately, the house we stayed in wasn't.

The house itself was nice enough, five minutes from the village with ample parking. Our room was on the top floor and had an en suite bathroom, just as we had expected. It was the decor that stopped us dead in our tracks. Think Chucky from the film Child's Play, meets Madeleine McCann, and you'll get an idea of what the massive (and I mean four feet by three kinds of massive), hand-painted portrait of a little girl was like. This monstrosity was leaning at an angle from the dado rail directly over our bed. The subject was cross-eyed and staring manically at us, baring its appalling smile at our every bounce of the mattress. I dared to move closer to read the signature in the corner. Yep, as I suspected, the artist was our landlady, and they had gone so far as to bolt the damned thing to the rail!

Further inspection of the bathroom and TV lounge disclosed more montages on each wall, of the grinning relatives of our hosts at various holiday locations. It was like being eyed up for dinner by a tribe of starving cannibals. So, we did what most people would do in that situation. Rather than complaining to the establishment, we reasoned it was only one night, so chose cowardice instead. Josh's new shirt was thrown over horror child and various bits of my clothing adorned the rest. Only then, with our entire wardrobe on the walls, could we finally relax.

We discovered to our further disappointment that not one restaurant in the village had any tables free. We called everyone and always got the same answer: "Sorry, we're full all evening."

Our fault, it was Saturday night after all, and we had forgotten to book. A takeaway it was then. We lay on the bed and started to research what was on offer locally.

"What do you fancy?" mused Josh, as he scrolled through the list of local food delivery places. I glanced sideways at him.

"*Hmmm*, I don't fancy anything heavy or overly spicy, so not Indian. Hey!" I stopped and grinned. "Do they do free deliverance?" I gestured at the leering creepy kid on the wall. Josh laughed.

"What about Chinese then?"

"No, not Chinese. We always regret it later when we feel too full and sickly," I reminded him.

Josh nodded in agreement.

"Thai! Light and not too spicy. Is there a Thai place here?"

Josh wasn't listening. Instead, he was looking at his phone, at a picture of what looked like a holy temple.

"Listen to this – there's a massive Buddhist temple about ten minutes away. You can have a free meditation session and they have a gift shop and café where they do breakfasts."

At hearing this, I perked up immediately, my mind already visualising myself lumbering and dragging back to the car like Jacob Marley, loaded down with strings of dangly bells and incense sticks.

"Gift shop?"

"Yeah, and breakfasts," Josh repeated, more interested in sausages and bacon than ornamental Buddhas. I didn't like to tell him that most Buddhists ate very little meat, if any at all. I figured I'd let him find out for himself. We decided to give it a go the following day. There wasn't much else to do as we'd already hobbled down most of the cobbles and nothing else seemed to be open on a Sunday.

As they say in books, the next morning dawned… and it was chucking it down. We packed our bags and ran the gauntlet of 'the family at Filey' photos in the hallway to the car. The hosts had already gone out for the day. As we passed, I noticed they'd tied a bag to the door handle – an amateur attempt at a trap in case we snooped in their private rooms. The threat of more family portraits would have deterred any potential burglar from entering anyway, but their Trip Advisor score immediately fell by another point.

Ten minutes later, we peered through the slashing rain and wildly swiping windscreen wipers at the most amazing golden palace I've ever seen. Surrounded by forest and within the grounds of an old stately home, it shone through the rain like a mirage of opulence and hope to all who gazed upon it. It had a gilded domed roof and a white stone pathway through lush green lawns to the door. We could see inside the glass walls. There were rows of deep red velvet chairs, plush carpeting, and a bank of enormous, bejewelled, gold statues facing the seats. They didn't appear short of a bob or two, these Buddhists.

The free meditation didn't start for another hour, so we headed for the café. I was right about the bacon. Josh ate his vegan cake and coffee breakfast with a stoicism brought on by the calming presence of orange-robed servers. £20 later, we had a mooch around the gift shop while we waited. Acrylic display stands sported offerings of mobile phone and laptop cases decorated with mandalas and lotus flower designs at eye-watering prices, all sporting stickers shamelessly admitting they were 'Made in China'. There were fewer dangling adornments in the shop than I expected – a sign of the times,

I guess. I reasoned that it's more politically correct to purchase phone covers than strung-up effigies of animals.

There was nothing we fancied buying, so giving ourselves five minutes' grace, we headed to the palace. I was excited to see inside properly, and it didn't disappoint, especially the under-floor heating, which I figured would dry our sodden coats off nicely while we meditated. A bald lady with buck teeth, wearing basic orange robes and black-rimmed spectacles, asked us quietly to remove our shoes. Josh and I *"ooohed"* and *"aaaaaahed",* as we padded around the room while others arrived, our socks sinking into the deep cream carpet. The statues of various Buddhist deities were even bigger and more impressive up close. Shimmering, as they caught the light from the windows, they were stunningly detailed, having been made by master craftsmen. But what were the Jaffa cakes all about? Josh and I made side-eyes at each other in amusement. Dotted all over the place were small piles of chocolate biscuits, Aldi's luxury marshmallows, Tunnocks' chocolate wafers, and bottles of cloudy lemonade. I could see Josh brightening up at the vague possibility that the meditation ended with pop and snacks.

Right on cue, a small door to the left opened, and a monk appeared. He was a small nut-brown man with a shaved head and orange and scarlet robes befitting his status. Adjusting his glasses (why do all monks appear to have poor eyesight?), and with a casual wave of his hand, he gestured for us to be seated, while the other hand appeared to be holding his robe closed. Everyone sat. His silence and utter calm demanded total obedience. What followed was a brief insight into what Buddhists believed in and worked towards, which is basically to do good deeds with a calm mind. I won't and can't give a lesson here on how to become a Buddhist as it takes a lifetime of learning, but I got the impression that meditating was extremely difficult and must take lots of practice. All the time my eyes were closed I was thinking, *What are the chocolate biscuits about*? And *Charlotte and Melanie would love this!* I couldn't empty my mind even for a second, but it was suddenly obvious this was exactly the peace I'd been seeking.

"But what has this to do with Mandy?" I hear you ask.

The peace of mind, that mellow, loving, cloud of connection I feel with Mandy, is what I aspire to carry as much as I can when I'm not on it. I felt the same kind of peace of mind and spiritual connection for a short while at the Buddhist Centre that day. Maybe that's what Simon had been searching for in his DMT experience, too. Not Buddhism, but the mindset that allows us to connect with whatever our souls need so they can flourish.

As we collected our steaming coats on the way out, I asked the lady in the robes what the biscuits and pop were all about. As no one had cracked any open, my curiosity had been piqued even more. Her reply had us chuckling with amusement.

"Oh, they're offerings to the monks. They don't *need* biscuits," she said. "It's just that people bring them as offerings, and they get shared out between them afterwards." I glanced at the piles of sweets and chocolate and wondered how these monks stayed so slim. I could feel Josh's dismay that he wouldn't be getting any.

I later learned that in Thailand, the monks visit the lay community each day and are given food to sustain them for the next twenty-four hours. They take out a bowl and villagers put in rice, fruit, maybe a bit of chicken, anything they can spare in exchange for wise teachings. It sounds fair enough, but I saw no evidence that in England the monks were given anything other than sweet stuff from their attendees. I returned home determined to find out more about Buddhism. I yearned to find *my* peaceful place.

Later that week I was out shopping and, having already found a Buddhist Centre near our home, had planned a visit. I was perusing the shelves of custard creams and stacks of ginger nuts when a sudden thought occurred to me. This was no way to offer to monks! All this sugar must surely play havoc with their skin and teeth. They must be sick of chocolate by now. *What do people eat in Tibet?*

'Aha!' I said to myself, smugly. 'Noodles!' I chucked a four-pack of Pot Noodle into my basket. A few days later, sitting in the meeting, my meditation was ruined by my constant inability to focus on anything other than my Chicken and Mushroom Pot Noodle pack, surrounded by a variety of McVities best behind the monk's head. It stuck out like a sore thumb. I made a mental note to stick to Fig Rolls next time.

After a few visits to the centre, however, I realised that I don't need to attend meetings and stick to one belief system to be a good and enlightened person. Even the 'spiritual' bohemian stance is constricting. It involves going to a variety of ceremonies and events, a certain uniform of hippie-style clothing, hours of meditation, a lot of lighting candles, and making meditative tributes and prayers to a whole history of Gods, Goddesses, Angels, and other deities I neither believed in nor could commit to.

A new 'medicine' accompanying the spiritual lifestyle currently is cacao, which is basically raw chocolate, blended with plant milk and natural sugars, on an empty stomach (Of course you'll experience a 'high' from that!). Josh and I both tried it, and whilst we thought it was pleasant, it didn't really do anything for us spiritually.

I quickly discovered that attempting to live within the constraints of this alternative lifestyle is limiting and financially difficult. I knew what I wanted – peace of mind and connection with others; I didn't need or want to feel that those desires were to become a full-time job. Don't get me wrong, I love the lifestyle, the people, the clothes, and the overall sense of freedom of it all, but sometimes I like to rock out to metal music, laugh at politically incorrect jokes, and binge-watch serial killer programmes on Netflix. I've found instead that you can take something from everyone you meet and, if it makes sense to you, then incorporate it into your life. I pop in and out of *Buddhism for Beginners* when I feel the need and try to remember to live in the present. Most of the people I spend time with are the same. Just ordinary people trying to live a good life.

IT'S GONNA BE ACID

Remember I said I'd tell you an LSD story? Charlotte is very interested in psychedelics. Unlike Melanie and Robin, who were happy with Mandy and DMT occasionally, Charlotte wanted to continue her journey with DMT and possibly then try Ayahuasca. I'm not so sure yet. I was very interested in Ayahuasca at the beginning of our journey with Mandy, but after thinking about it, I would need a lot more experience with psychedelics before I committed to a potentially twelve-hour, mind-blowing trip I can't get out of. Again, I feel Mandy is enough for me and gives me all I need.

Charlotte has been to raves and taken ecstasy and LSD/acid when she was a teenager, and again, I never knew about it, so when I told her we could get LSD gel tabs, she was more than up for it. I had only tried it once before and it was in the form of a couple of cardboard tabs with a drop of LSD liquid on them. From the design, we worked out they'd been in storage for a while, but Josh and I gave them a shot at a campsite in Bridlington. I expected no end of beautiful visuals as we strolled around the field, but all I saw was the ground looking a little swampy as I walked on it. I was thinking, *these are crap,* until I looked closely at a fence post and watched pink and green waves undulating up and around it.

"Quick!" I whispered eagerly to Josh. "Take a photo!" Such is the gormless brain on acid. It wore off quickly, and, unimpressed, we never considered it again until much later.

I thought about it for a while though and decided that if she was up for it, I'd give it another go. I also wanted Charlotte to be there when I took my first LSD gel tabs. She was experienced, and I trusted her to know what to do to ensure a pleasant trip. I had kept a photo on my phone of Charlotte at a rave somewhere. It was taken at night time: she had both arms in the air, her hair in a messy bun, and wearing a jacket with the words 'It's Gonna Be Acid' in bright yellow across the back. Yep, she was my best choice of companion for the event. I checked I was free for the next few weekends and then called her to see if she fancied a night away in an Airbnb apartment around ten miles away. I figured it would be nice to have a girlie night away from other distractions, just me and her, and a few acid tabs. We chose a weekend in late October and booked ourselves in.

It was falling dark around 5:30 p.m. in October, so it was the perfect environment. The apartment was one Josh and I had stayed in a couple of times when we had been at house parties and had been unable to drive home. It was well equipped with breakfast stuff and had a beautiful, enclosed courtyard with fairy lights and natural stonework – lots of visual stimulation for us to focus on. Brian, who owned it, had living quarters next door and was a sweet guy, so it seemed the ideal place to chill out and enjoy some psychedelic experimentation. His annexe had a connecting door that led to his dining room, but it was locked and curtained off for total privacy. Bless Charlotte, she was so touched I wanted to share the evening with her, and she assured me she would be supportive of what was to be my first genuine experience with some decent LSD.

Josh drove us there in the late afternoon with the arrangement that Adz would share the driving and pick us up the next morning. Josh had compiled a playlist of movies he wanted to watch, which comprised Four-Headed Shark, Three-Headed Shark, Two-Headed Shark, and, well, Shark I guess, the local takeaway was on speed dial, and he had a couple of mates online to play games with in the interim. We'd suggested that he pop up to see Adz, but the guys so rarely had evenings to themselves that Josh was more than happy to have an entire night to do man stuff on his own.

Charlotte and I were super giddy. I had four tabs of LSD in my jeans pocket. A tab commonly comes as a tiny square of cardboard with a cartoon or psychedelic design and a drop of LSD soaked into it. These were gel capsules – a full drop of pure LSD in a tiny dissolvable bubble, carefully sourced from a reputable seller Josh had found online. We agreed that we'd be sensible and take one each to start with.

Josh waved us off and drove away, ready for his peaceful night in, and we let ourselves into the apartment. As I expected, there was bread, fruit, and cereal in the kitchen, and a comfy sofa complete with enormous cushions and a couple of fluffy, dove grey blankets over each arm. Everything we needed for the perfect night. It was just dropping dusk, and the evening was fine but cool, so we grabbed the blankets and got snuggled up on the outside chairs with a glass of lemonade each. Again, we were sensible and just had soft drinks so as not to spoil the effect of the LSD. Our environment was so pretty and peaceful and we felt that we'd chosen well. Strings of fairy lights twinkled around the walls, shining pinks, greens, and yellows in the dark. It was quite magical. We put some mellow music on our phones and chatted and laughed quietly for a while, then it was time. Of course, we had to take the obligatory acid-tab-on-tongue selfie, so after grinning away a few times for the perfect shot, we each moved the first tab under our tongues and waited, smiling happily with anticipation. We waited some more… Nothing… I had never been so underwhelmed. Charlotte was fiddling and faffing around with the music, and we carried on chatting, occasionally pausing to check how much time had elapsed and to glance at each other to see if anything was happening. Ages had passed and it was now half-past seven and two hours since we'd had the first tab. I checked the internet.

"*Hmmm*, it says here that we should feel the effects after twenty minutes. It's been two hours now."

Charlotte looked doubtful.

"Yeah, I was expecting a lot more after all this time. I'm pretty sure it didn't take this long the last time I had it." She frowned slightly. "Shall we wait a bit longer though, just in case it's a slow-working one?"

She knew a lot better than I did, so I agreed.

I admit I was a bit disappointed, though. I thought to myself that if this is what Woodstock attendees were going wild on, they must have been a right set of lightweight pansies! I gave it another ten minutes. It was only 7:40 but pitch black by then and I was so desperate I was listening to Westlife!

"I think that after over two hours nothing is gonna happen," I reasoned to Charlotte, peering at her through the dark.

I referenced the expertise of Google again, throwing in a few Reddit comments for good measure.

"Everyone on here says it should have been working ages ago. I reckon we have the last two," I concluded firmly.

We were stone-cold sober, and it was approaching eight o'clock. After a few more *"ummms", "aaaaaahs", "dunnos"*, and a few more searches online, we threw caution to the wind and popped the last two under our tongues, accepting that the first tabs may have been duds. At a tenner a tab, I was already mentally working out my indignant email of complaint to the supplier in the morning.

"Do you know what?" said Charlotte a little while later. "I need some cigarettes. Is there a shop around here?" This surprised me as Charlotte stopped smoking a couple of years previously. I didn't want to encourage her to start again.

"You don't need cigs," I told her. "Anyway, I've no idea where there's a shop. There's a pub across the road, but they don't sell cigs anymore."

We fell into quiet contemplation of our surroundings.

"Can you feel anything yet?" I asked.

She shrugged her shoulders. "Not really, a few wavy colours, but that could be the fairy lights. I do need some cigs, though. Can we go find a shop?"

I had a quick think.

"Okay, let me give Jackie a quick call. She only lives up the road, so she'll know where the closest shop is."

I had a quick natter with Jackie, whose house parties we'd been to, and she confirmed there was a shop open about ten minutes' walk away. It was dark but still only a quarter past eight, so we set off in the direction she told us.

The night sky was crisp and clear, and the house lights were bright and sparkly as we walked. It felt like I was walking along a street in a video game. All the colours were vibrant and quite beautiful. Cars drove by with blinding headlights, and I could feel the LSD kicking in. It felt great! In the distance, I could see someone walking toward us.

"I'll ask this chap if he knows where the shop is," I told Charlotte. "Just to make sure we're heading in the right direction."

She clung to my arm and peered wild-eyed down the road.

"Mum, there's no one there," she hissed.

I looked harder.

"There!" I pointed at the approaching figure. "You just can't see because of the shadows. It's a fella."

She clawed at my sleeve. "It isn't!" she squeaked, her voice catching in a manic whisper. "It's the acid, there's no one there, keep walking."

She began dragging me along. I stopped the chap as he walked by, Charlotte still pulling me away.

"Excuse me?"

He looked like he was probably a bit of a lad, but was polite enough. He didn't know where the shop was, so hopping on one leg to counter Charlotte's heaving, I let him go on his way and we carried on up the road.

"Give up! There's nothing to worry about, it's half-past eight, and there are kids still up at this time, stop worrying!"

I could see families watching the telly through the windows of the houses we passed. I was enjoying the surreal feeling and was happily pointing out stars and pretty lights to Charlotte, who was white-faced, eyes darting about nervously as if she was expecting something supernatural was about to leap from the doorway of Londis and snatch her.

"Come on!" I encouraged. "Look, there's someone else coming."

Charlotte reared back in panic.

"*Wahhhhhh!* There's nobody there, Mum. You're seeing things!"

I'd had enough of this carry-on and was getting impatient. As the (very pleasant and normal looking) man passed us, I asked again if he knew where the shop was. He did and kindly directed us to the top of the road. Charlotte refused to make eye contact with her perception of this non-existent person, and started digging her fingers into my arm and pulling me away, muttering to him, "Thank you, we're okay, you're not real, goodbye."

Maybe it was time to give up on the cigarettes and go back to the apartment. Being outside obviously wasn't the right thing for Charlotte. We'd only gone about two hundred yards, but it was clear she wasn't going to go much further, what with all the goblins and Slender Man characters lurking in the dark of the dual carriageway, waiting to drag her kicking and screaming to the dark side. We turned back.

"Come on," I soothed. "Look, we're nearly back. There's the gate."

I could hear her talking quietly behind me, phone to her ear, but couldn't make out what she was saying.

"Who are you talking to?" I asked.

"Adz? No, I'm okay, keep talking to me," she was whispering. "I'm fine, I'm just a bit… I need you to talk me down."

Oh, marvellous. I knew that if Adz thought she wasn't having a good time, he would be coming within minutes to take her home.

"Stop it, Charlotte! You're fine, we're back now. You don't need to be calling Adz." I admit I was pissed off with her by that point. "You're bringing the vibe down," I growled. "Put the phone down and let's sit out for a bit."

No, she wasn't having any of it, but at least she ended the call.

"I'm going to sit inside," she insisted indignantly, wrapping the blanket around her, and going into the living room to sit on the sofa. I was so mad. We had both looked forward to this for ages and there she was, acting like a crazy person. I felt great and was beginning to enjoy the waves of colour from the lights and dancing patterns on the stone wall.

"God!" I chuntered to myself.

Hang on… what's that noise? I froze and listened intently for a moment.

"Josh, Josh? It's me! Mum's gone mental; she's seeing things. You HAVE to come and help. I don't know what to do!"

Charlotte was on the phone with Josh. I shot up.

"Get off that phone! You don't need him coming over; it'll ruin his night. You've had some acid and you're just a bit overwhelmed."

She hung up and rolled around in the blanket, looking quite bonkers.

"I'm going back out," I told her firmly. "Do NOT call anyone else. Try to calm down, then come out when you're ready and we'll sit and enjoy the rest of the evening, okay?"

She nodded and closed her eyes. *Phew!* I sat back in the garden and tried to regain some of my previous feelings of euphoria.

"Josh! I'm serious, PLEASE come! We need help!" Tiny screeches came again from inside.

My eyes popped open.

"What the actual fuck, Charlotte!?"

I was halfway out of my seat to go and wrestle her to the floor in a headlock when it went silent, and my phone rang. It was Josh.

"Don't come!" I blurted out before he could speak. "We're perfectly okay; she's just having some issues seeing invisible people, but I'm absolutely fine."

I was desperate to convince him he didn't need to come out to rescue us.

"You can hear I'm fine. I've no idea why she's saying I've gone mad; it's obvious that I haven't."

Josh knows me and agreed that I seemed okay, but that he'd come anyway as he hadn't started watching the movies and he wanted to support me in dealing with Charlotte. Inside the house, I could hear: "Josh, are you there? Josh, you need to come. Hello? Hello?" from Charlotte, frantically whispering into the engaged phone tone. I rolled my eyes and sighed in defeat.

"Okay, love, drive safely and we'll see you in around thirty minutes." Hanging up, I went inside, closing the door behind me.

"Right," I snapped peevishly. "Josh is coming, and he'll be here soon. You need to calm down."

I then employed the standard repertoire of care for the situation and put my arms around her. Her head poked out of the grey blanket, and she whimpered pitifully.

"You've taken acid," I reminded her.

"You're having a bad trip but you're safe. You're in an Airbnb with me and Josh is coming."

"Yes, yes." She nodded. "Don't go out again, Mum," she begged. She was pink in the face and sweating in the blanket.

I was feeling sorry for her by then. She wasn't having a good time at all. I rocked her gently as she relaxed a bit and kept repeating clearly and firmly that she was safe, and that it was just an acid trip. So far, so good, and it might have been until…

Bang bang!

"Hello!"

A grinning face appeared in the glass door panel.

"I've just come to see if you have enough bread and things." It was Brian, the owner, coming to check on us. I patted

Charlotte, who was now reassuringly quiet, and got up to answer the door.

"Hi!" I smiled. "Do you want to co—"

"*Waaaaaaahhhhhhh!* Fuck offfffffff! Get oooooouuuuut!"

Brian leapt back with a yelp, as if his balls had been tasered. I turned around, hand still on the handle of the half-opened door to see Charlotte partly immobilised by the cocooning blanket, screeching and trying to escape caterpillar-wise over the back of the sofa. Her face was contorted with terror.

"Muuuuuuuum! *Aaaaaaaaahhh!*"

Shit! Think, fast!

"Sorry about this," I stammered to Brian, who had backed away and was now standing feet from the door. Bent over, he was staring in goggle-eyed fascination at this crazy part human part blanket thing writhing on his best Ikea sofa. "I'll come out."

Big mistake.

"Nooooooooooo! Muuuuuuuuuum! Don't go out!" she shrieked even louder. "*Aaaaaaaaaaah!*"

Charlotte rolled and writhed like some horrific pupae from The Fly. *Oh my God, now what to do?*

"I'm *so* sorry," I muttered through a centimetre of the open door. "She's very stressed and came away for a rest. She gets upset, and…"

I shut the door. There was no explaining what poor Brian was witnessing. *Come on, Josh!* I needed him to do some damage limitation, if that was at all possible.

I untangled Charlotte from the blanket in which she was swaddled and assured her the evil zombie had gone and that Josh would soon be here. Fortunately, within the next ten minutes, Josh was quietly opening the door. He was a welcome and sensible presence in the mayhem. I quickly updated him.

"Right, you need to have a word with Brian and think of some reason, any believable reason, for Charlotte acting like that. If he realises she's on drugs, we can never come here again."

I was worried as we liked the place.

"Are you alright?" he asked Charlotte, who was still lying on the sofa mumbling.

He went and sat next to her and gave her a hug, which seemed to do the trick. She sprung to life, hugging him and begging him to stay, saying he made her feel safe. It's testimony to Josh's consistent reliability that she trusted not Adz, her partner, not me, her mum, but Josh to guard her against all the evil the acid could throw at her. After a few more hugs, he managed to pry her hands from his arm and pop next door to see Brian. It wasn't long before he reappeared.

"Sorted." He smiled. "It was fine. I just apologised and told him that Charlotte has a very stressful job working with adults with challenging behaviour and that she's come away to unwind. I explained that when he knocked on the door, it was unfortunate that she was in the middle of a full-blown panic attack. It was just bad timing and she's okay now."

Brilliant though it was, there was a flaw in this, such as how in God's name did Brian imagine she'd be back at work every Monday after spending her weekends mentally destroyed? But hey-ho. Most explanations for bizarre occurrences don't bear close scrutiny. I slumped in relief. It seemed that yet again, Josh had saved our collective bacon.

Between us, we got Charlotte to lie down on the only double bed. She refused to let go of Josh, so he lay at the side of her making apologetic and bemused faces at me, while she muttered, and half-dozed. It seemed the screaming and panic were over, at least. Jackie called back to say she was with Melanie at a party and did we manage to find the shop? I gave her a quick rundown, and she laughed.

"Leave them to it, get a taxi and come to the party."

I couldn't but I thanked her, anyway. In all honesty, it would have been a great idea. The drug in me was seeking stimulation and in a darkened, quiet apartment, I stalked about anxiously.

For the next couple of hours, we monitored Charlotte and chatted quietly. Of course, eventually, we got tired, and it appeared that Charlotte was falling asleep, so Josh moved to the sofa, and I got into bed with her. As I dozed off, I congratulated myself on remembering to keep repeating loudly and firmly to Charlotte, reminding her, "You're on acid." I'd done the right thing. I sighed sleepily. Just as my eyes closed and I drifted into a deep, deep sleep, I vaguely remembered the connecting door to Brian's house... right behind the sofa!

The next morning, we dropped Charlotte off before Adz had to come and pick her up. She had the good grace to look sheepish. She had a lot of explaining to do and even more laughs at her expense to deal with. Poor acid expert Charlotte still hasn't lived it down. She vowed never to touch drugs again, ever, not even paracetamol. She *so* will – she's a rebel. It might take a while, though. What is interesting is that she and I are the same weight, had eaten the same food, and had the same number of tabs in the same environment. I'd say that's some proof that drugs affect people differently. I also reckon Ayahuasca is now off the agenda.

That same Christmas I found an online seller who made me a smiling gingerbread ornament holding a little sign, and I hung it on Charlotte's tree when she wasn't looking. The sign said, *I'm not a Biscuit, you're on ACID*. There's still a lot of mileage in it yet!

THE END OF THE BEGINNING

Mandy/ecstasy isn't dubbed 'the love drug' for nothing. The human condition is genetically geared toward procreation and the sensual feelings accompanying Mandy only serve to heighten that desire. Of course, not toward everyone you meet, but with the right partner, sex can be either a spiritual or lust-filled sensation fest. Sex and love are not necessarily the same thing at all. But they can be in some circumstances. On Mandy the *'phwoar'*! factor can also be dumbed down into thinking, "*Mmmm*, I'd like to touch you all over because you feel *so* good" and cuddling up to your object of desire – be it a man, woman, or total stranger and possibly their dog. What Josh tells me is that for him, the erection he first experienced on Mandy hasn't happened for a while. He believes that Mandy allowed him total and complete release and that it doesn't happen now because he's not as repressed as he was.

Talking of dogs, they are the most loyal of sitters when on any recreational drug. I know our dachshund Rory can sense and probably see quite clearly that his Master and Mistress are on it again and need protection from any stupid ideas they may have. During our campouts, Rory plonks himself on a blanket at our feet, stays put for the duration, and sighs at us occasionally. On the upside, he can root through any food left around, as none of the campers on Mandy has any appetite. I recall Rory taking me and my sparkly eyes for a stroll around a campsite at three in the morning hunting for abandoned tubes of Pringles and half-eaten sausage rolls. He carefully steered me around the trip hazard of invisible guy ropes like a burglar with his eye on the glass cabinet housing the Hope diamond.

Maybe it's different for everyone, but for Josh and me, by the time sex is thought about again, it's around five in the morning when people start heading back to their van, tent, or room in total exhaustion. Sex, when I'm one eye asleep, is off the agenda, full stop. Men, however, appear to be able to muster one last surge for copulation, in the manner of the last gasp of a drowning man going under. The usual dialogue between me and Josh goes something like this:

"Babe?"

Here we bloody go.

"What?"

"Do you fancy, y'know, snuggles?"

"Do I heck, it's five o'clock in the morning! Get yourself to sleep, I'm knackered," I reply, turning on my side to face away from him.

"Yeah, but go on, just a little bit," he begs, poking me in the kidneys with what feels like a broom handle.

I'll likely be rolling my eyes in the dark and getting angry.

"Babe, stop it now, I'm tired, we have to get some sleep, it's already morning and we'll feel terrible tomorrow if we don't. You always do this, it's alright for you, just go to sleep for God's sake."

I bide my time and around five minutes after his whining ceases, I tentatively turn over and peek at him through half-closed pretending-to-be-asleep-eyes. All I see is a gaping mouth from whence the nagging came, and, *"Zzzzzzzzzzzzzzzzzz"*

Game over.

Josh and I had sex when we were on half a pill at home. It was fun; it was beautifully romantic, and it was quick. I guess it was exactly what we needed at the time and we both ended up smiling and happy. It's a strange choice, and one we may well change soon, but Josh and I don't tend to have Mandy on our own much. To me, it's a very social drug. We found it, or it found us when we needed to connect with other people. I feel it would be wasting it on just the two of us, as Josh and I are deep talkers and are good at connecting without stimulants. Maybe that's being smug or dismissive, I don't know. I reckon that sex and the love vibe with Mandy are intermingled, in that both involve touch, encourage a connection of emotions, and a relaxation of both body and mind. Of course, you can spend the days after regretting sex with a stranger, but in my experience, it's no more of a risk with Mandy than it is after alcohol. And too much of both can result in a jelly cannon, anyway.

Melanie and Robin, however, regularly enjoy Mandy as a couple and have so much fun, just the two of them. Once they told us they dressed up in fancy dress and had a 'goth night' together. They say it allows them to have an intimate escape from their admittedly very busy lives and just enjoy each other. I love that idea, but I'm not sure it would work for us in the same way. I think because I'm such a social butterfly, and can talk and dance for the entire night, I'm concerned I'd be bored or irritated. This is because Josh comes up on Mandy, talks, socialises, and then like a spent firework fizzles and flops (well, parts of him do, see section above). He then sits with eyes closed, smiling away at whatever is going on in his head and doesn't move again. He can do this for hours as the event just carries on around him. If that were to happen with just the two of us, I couldn't cope with being the only one dancing and talking rubbish to myself. Mind you, Josh has tentatively started dancing a little bit. I reckon Mandy matches your mood, so maybe if he's more active he'll stay engaged longer, we shall see.

I had questions about Mandy, too. Most I know the answer to now, like, how did I miss out on the recreational drug scene? It was there and extremely prevalent in the youth subculture of the late seventies, then later in the rave scene of the late eighties and early nineties, but although I was an adult, I simply hadn't grown up. Throughout those periods I had children; I had husbands; I had a mortgage; I paid rent and worked many jobs. Inside, I was still a child, though. When I think back, I hadn't a clue what I was doing or where my life was going. My judgments and prejudices were formed during those years, as were my long-term relationships with family and friends. It is no surprise that by the time I grew up, faced with losing the love and respect of my children, I was essentially starting again from scratch.

All the while, life for teenagers and young people of my age was happening around me. While I changed nappies and checked into Women's Refuges, other teenagers danced, went to concerts and discos with their friends, and shopped in giggling groups at Tammy Girl. I made my bed, as my mum would tell me frequently, but I was once told, and I still believe, you must live your young life sometime. Unfortunately for me, it came late and at a price. I can't say for sure that experimenting with drugs would have been part of my life had I lived as a normal teenager, but my personality has always been geared toward 'doing stuff' so I can imagine it would.

When I was at school in 1978, a girl in my class ran away from home and was found in London weeks later, dead from an overdose of heroin. The news rocked our village and was the source of gossip for a long while. Back then, any heroin-related story was big news and something that only happened in faraway London. A fourteen-year-old from a few streets away being involved with it was unheard of. Sadly, though, shameful rumours abounded that she came from a poor family, had a rough upbringing, and was a scruff – anything to distance the locals from the undesirables who took drugs. She was an ordinary child from an ordinary family! Even now, heroin terrifies me, which shows that drugs still made an impact on me even back then. They were just used by people far away, and neither parents nor children could relate.

What I wish was that I'd discovered Mandy much sooner. I've been drunk and been sick. I've been drunk and done things I'm ashamed of, but with Mandy, I have, at worst, felt reflective and, at best, euphoric and healed. Sometimes I question whether I could live life from this moment without ever having a relationship with Mandy again.

I think about suddenly being unable to source Mandy. I'd get used to it because I'd have to. Would I seek the same feeling in something else? Would I just move on with the new me? The lessons I have learned from Mandy have been lasting in that I still seek connections with strangers but not so desperately (Josh still occasionally tells me not to be so 'in your face'). I have yet to fully master letting friendships develop at a normal pace. I've learned how different I feel when truly relaxed and able to let go. Mandy broke down social barriers for both Josh and me. Now we would be the ones to talk to a stranger on their own at a party. Certainly, we still want people to spend time with, but don't worry as much about people not liking us or judging us. Mandy opened the door for us to be ourselves. We have made quite a few friends whom we only ever see at gatherings with other mutual friends. It's almost like a Mandy family. Are they real friends? For the time we are in their vicinity, yes. Real, lasting friends are, as in any other situation, much harder to find.

My friend Dawn has never taken drugs of any kind. I met her when I bought a cupboard off eBay and collected it from her house. She has no hobbies to speak of. Doesn't listen to music, doesn't read much, she's a mum and wife and is happy doing just that. It saddens me that we don't see each other much or go out together and make memories to share due to her various health, and, I suspect, confidence issues. Her ability to lip-read is outstanding, and most people don't know she's deaf until she tells them. She is another one who would benefit from the connection Mandy has to offer. If she's honest, I think she's utterly bemused by me. Our friendship ticks along without us even trying and I can talk to her about anything.

I still wish for close friends, but am no longer so needy that I allow others to mistreat me. I have a handful of good friends now who I share fun and activities with and we make memories together that are unrelated to Mandy, but who I wouldn't have met before, because of a lack of confidence. Josh and I have found that a way of approaching connections is to do it one event at a time. If we chat with strangers on a night out, then that's brilliant, and it's enough. Their company alone would make that one night special. If we don't see them again, the enjoyment of that night doesn't change. There may then be another opportunity, on another day, to connect with someone completely different. Josh and I travel our journey one day at a time – and so does everyone else. I had an epiphany one Wednesday when I was out dog walking. It hit me that love truly is stronger than we know. I understood that now I am blessed with love from friends and family and with the lessons Mandy taught me, I was able to become the best version of myself and love without reservation in return.

Josh and I thought we'd struck gold when we were introduced to a past acquaintance of Robin. I began chatting with her on social media and we discovered we shared a love of seventies music and all things retro. Before COVID, Suzie ran dance nights in village halls, both as a male and then after her gender surgery. Suzie was a transgender lady, tall and very shy. She transitioned very late at age forty-eight and had been married to Alison – slight and tomboy in appearance, with elfin features and who is a biological woman, for ten years. Alison was the loveliest lady ever. If there was such a thing as a sweet soul, Alison was it. She left her home and friends in America and now lived to make Suzie happy, deferring to her on almost every subject. Her support for Suzie and her transition was total, although it can't have been easy. After all, she married a man and was now in what society in general would view as a lesbian relationship.

We saw photos of Alison from the year before Suzie's transition and she was a pretty girl with shoulder-length hair that she had now cut very short. She wore jeans and tops with no makeup or jewellery. In contrast, Suzie wore makeup, coloured her hair, and wore rings and bracelets and pretty tops. They lived around two hours' drive from us, and we hit it off immediately. We had a group chat on social media where Josh, Alison, Suzie, and I would natter most of the day. Josh occasionally warned me not to get close too fast, but I was too far gone to listen. I had a friend and in fairness – he loved them, too. Suzie and I would talk for hours on the phone, so after a while, we arranged a visit to stay over at theirs one weekend.

Suzie was lovely natured, but sometimes hard to read. She avoided making eye contact with us at first. Josh and I took some Mandy for us all, which eased any first-meeting awkwardness, and we had a wonderful time. We loved their house, which was chaotic and homely. It had a real hippie vibe with hanging plants, vegan cookbooks on every surface, amateur sculptures, and a painting of Alison done by an American friend of hers a few months before. It showed Alison directing a large round electric fan at a hummingbird that battled mid-flight with delicate and exhausted wings against the blast of air. On reflection, that painting summed up

Alison's situation perfectly. Constantly pushing away her femininity and now hidden behind a far greater force in Suzie, she was powerless to help herself. I remember a conversation we had on that first visit while Suzie was in the shower.

"Suzie needs people around her, people who support and understand her," said Alison. "She had a friend called Heather who was amazing, she went to all Suzie's doctor and hospital appointments with her, visited her, went places with her, they were best friends for over six years," Alison recounted sadly.

"Okay, so what happened?" I asked. I admit I already felt slightly jealous of this amazing ex-friend and was secretly glad she was out of the picture.

"Well, one day I was tired as I work full time and look after the house. Suzie has always been bad at that kind of stuff. Heather came around and said to Suzie, 'I think you need to consider Alison a bit more. She's working full-time and is always supporting you. Maybe if you just made her a meal or something when she gets home, it would be a big help to her.'"

I nodded; it was a fair comment. Even from our short friendship, I noticed that whilst she was now a woman, Suzie stuck rigidly to archaically assigned gender roles when it came to housework.

"So don't ever say anything like that to her because she stormed off up to the bedroom and hasn't spoken to Heather since that day."

She went on to tell us that Suzie had had friends before, that had dropped off once the novelty value of having a transgender friend had worn off. This shocked me, but we agreed to tread carefully. That conversation was, in essence, a warning. I wish so much that I'd asked how recently it had happened, because if I had, it may have prepared me for what happened later.

For about six months, our friendship was everything I had hoped for. We talked and laughed, and I felt my life was now full. However, little things crept in that bothered us. When we met face to face, I discovered Suzie was a continuous weed smoker and was reliant on prescription painkillers. The combination often made her appear spaced-out and permanently stoned. At times like this, she would suffer paranoia and obsess over problems. She would randomly disappear for days, often weeks on end, ignoring messages or texts, often mid-conversation. She told us she had health issues relating to her surgery and was on a lot of different medications. It was clear that was true, and we were incredibly supportive. No matter how long she ignored us, we would be there.

Alison sat for days and nights on her own when Suzie would take herself off to bed to be alone, and we would chat with her and keep her company. Of course, it was likely depression that Suzie was suffering from, and I was there for her. We talked for hours on the phone, when *she* wanted to talk. If she didn't want to talk, I simply didn't exist. She once called out of the blue saying she felt suicidal, and that Alison was at work. Josh immediately called his boss and got the afternoon off, and we drove at a moment's notice to go see and check on her. Upon pulling up outside her house two hours later, we could see her through the window, dressed in her disco outfit, dancing to her Motown music without a care in the world.

We spoke at length to Alison on many occasions who loyally told us, "Suzie needs to know you're there even if she ignores you, so keep messaging."

This was all well and good, but if *we* needed support or even just a normal chat, Suzie wasn't there for us. Sending unacknowledged messages into the ether, even though Suzie was posting on her social media, was depressing and hurtful. Everything was on her terms. Alison told us many times about how worried and upset she was, but swore us to secrecy, so we just had to put up with it.

On another visit, Josh set Suzie and Alison up with a movie streaming service, because Suzie loved watching films. He installed a pair of speakers in her spare room so she could have music. Suzie couldn't praise him enough. She would comment on what a lovely, big-hearted, genuine guy Josh was – until suddenly she decided he wasn't.

Suzie had been blanking any contact for around three weeks. As had become usual, Josh and I had spent most of that time feeling anxious and worried about her. In the meantime, we did our best at supporting Alison. One day, a message from Suzie came up on the group chat. There was no "Hi, how are you doing?" What followed was a page's long diatribe about the government, why we should take a drug called Ivermectin to cure COVID, and that she had ordered herself some from the internet. Josh and I are certainly not averse to alternative ideas, but considering that Suzie was already on a cocktail of medication, we were concerned.

I asked her, "Have you checked with the hospital that it's okay to take Ivermectin? What if it reacts with your other meds?"

The reply came back quickly.

"I'm not sure I like how this conversation is going," she retorted. "I don't think I want to talk to you about this!"

Annoyed, I responded, "Suzie, I've waited weeks to talk to you. I've missed you. I don't deserve this."

No reply. I was well and truly in the doghouse. Another week of silence and my messages being ignored ensued. Josh and I were now losing patience.

The next time we heard from Suzie was a week later, and it was another screenshot about Ivermectin. Again, no asking how we were or any attempt at normal conversation. Josh replied to her this time. He told her he'd read the information on Ivermectin, he was open to it, and it was due to be trialled as a cure for COVID. He told her we had no objection to learning about any new ideas regarding cures for COVID, and if the trials were good, then it would be approved. After explaining that our only concern was for her, as she had health problems already, he then asked how she was. Suzie didn't reply and never spoke to Josh again. She would ignore his messages and treat him as though he didn't exist. Josh was confused about what he had done to offend her and was upset, so I called her to ask. She had no hesitation in telling me she found him dismissive and had no intention of speaking to him again, telling me to make something up if he asked what she'd said.

We'd tolerated months of pandering to Suzie's every whim, worrying if we'd upset her. We'd been side-lined and ignored whenever she felt like it. We had become Alison – mere satellites around planet Suzie. I'd had enough. With a heavy heart, I told her it couldn't continue. Josh had been nothing but kind to her and deserved better. He was my husband, and I wouldn't allow her to treat him that way. In true Suzie style, she simply responded that she didn't wish to discuss it further and disappeared. A couple of weeks later, I messaged Alison. Something had been bothering me.

"Hi, Alison. I need to tell you, before you lump us in with the people you say saw Suzie as a novelty, that the reason Suzie and I cannot be friends is nothing to do with her being transgender. It has everything to do with how we felt increasingly anxious and upset. Being continually ignored and then her blanking Josh, who has done nothing but be kind to you both, made the friendship impossible to sustain. I love you both and wish you all the happiness in the world. Please don't worry, I don't expect a reply. Be happy, Alison."

As predicted, I received no reply, although I could see the message had been read – maybe by Suzie herself, who knows?

What I do know is that Suzie had previously banned Alison from messaging those she'd fallen out with, including her daughter from a past relationship. I hadn't wished to cause further problems by making Alison feel an obligation to respond.

Oddly, I felt little but liberation. It was a shame, and I still think of Suzie often, but I could not end up in another controlling friendship like the one I'd had with Denise all those years ago. I thought it interesting when, a week or so later, Robin told me he'd seen on social media that Suzie was organising a seventies disco in a hall in their local town, and Suzie's ex-friend Heather had ticked that she was going. It seems obvious now that I was a replacement for Heather, and with me gone, Suzie had resumed contact with her once more. Suzie needs someone to fawn over her, after all. I haven't heard from either Suzie or Alison since.

It took a while for me to realise that not everyone who uses Mandy is necessarily bonded with you in every other way. Josh is sometimes concerned that the only people we meet now are connected by recreational drugs, and that normal and natural friendships are still difficult to make. He's partially correct, but I now have the confidence to try to make friends

– something I lacked before meeting Mandy. Once the glow has worn off, however, I still need to connect on other levels in the real world. Mandy doesn't turn arseholes overnight into spiritual gurus and your best mates. Come the morning, they are still arseholes. Mandy only opens the doors. What you find on the other side is for you to either keep or discard.

Aware too that so many of our connections were reliant upon Melanie and Robin arranging get-togethers, last summer Josh arranged a camp, which was a great success. Of course, almost all were originally friends of Melanie and Robin, but we're quickly becoming part of the group now, and hopefully, we will continue to meet people who may just become closer friends. I know that if we announce a camp or gathering, the number of people who are suddenly our friends increases, but according to Melanie, that's normal. I've come to accept that close friendships happen slowly and naturally, not as a result of stargazing and holding hands, wide-eyed on Mandy.

Talking of wide eyes and friendships, a perfect example was at a friend's surprise fortieth birthday party. Her husband had invited previous camp attendees, based on one meeting only. One girl at the party was very quiet and had never tried Mandy before. She didn't engage with anyone at all, and we could see she was out of her comfort zone in a room with a lot of strangers. When Melanie offered her a pill, she cautiously accepted. Within half an hour, she was holding both mine and Melanie's hands, hugging us and telling us all her life story, including her wish to have more love and connection in her life and to socialise more. This is familiar territory to both Melanie and me. It's pretty much par for the course with Mandy. It was a lovely couple of hours, seeing her so open and free, chatting and laughing. Before we left, the girl added us both on social media, hugging us and promising to keep in touch. A couple of days later, she put up a post on her Facebook page, just something random, so I liked the post and did a short but upbeat reply. For over two weeks, she was carrying on as normal on Facebook, but never once acknowledged my input, so I lessened my responses. Once upon a time I would have been upset and slighted by this, but now, even though it's disappointing, I recognise it as 'sesh-friends' syndrome. At another party with Mandy, she'd be chatting away again as if she'd known us for years. Without Mandy, she's still the same person with the same issues as she was before. It doesn't make her a bad person, and it doesn't mean she doesn't like us. In fairness, she doesn't know us. Mandy opened the door, but for the moment she is letting it swing shut behind her.

Baz and Poppy only use Mandy infrequently, usually when it's gifted, or traded – usually with us, Robin, or Melanie. They recently both left their jobs, and around the time of their discovery of DMT, ventured into spirituality as personal therapy, and then as a business. After knowing Poppy for a while, we observed that she wasn't half as naïve and delicate as our first impressions had implied. As we got to know her, we learned that she was something of a chameleon. She swapped intermittently between being overtly spiritual, and then binge-watching episodes of Friends. I discovered later that she was still finding her way, as she gradually transitioned into wearing the tasselled skirts and ankle bracelets, which were befitting of her future plans. Equally suited to the main drag in Ibiza when we first met, Poppy had had a hard upbringing, and finding spirituality was her way of dealing with her past.

They quickly began taking courses on Reiki, hosting cacao ceremonies and meditation groups, among other so-called spiritual pursuits. It became apparent that they would bond with other like-minded people as a result of starting to run their own business, and that we couldn't always be there to support them. We enjoy their company and wish them well, but we also understand that we need to establish other interests in common for friendships to last. In time, it became apparent to Josh and me that it was going to be difficult to be both friends *and* customers. Financially, we couldn't afford to. What we, and most people, need is a variety of friends outside the recreational drugs scene to feel fully whole and rounded. We do pop over to see Baz and Poppy for the occasional evening and always have a great time, but now mostly see them at Kirtans (groups where people sit and bang drums, play the guitar, and join in with singing spiritual songs). Baz still wants me to enjoy the full experience of a mushroom trip with him and is growing some of his own that he swears will do the trick. I had five grams with him in a cup of cacao, to no effect at all, but the last time I had one gram of a different variety and had the most amazing visuals like those of a DMT trip. I may continue to experiment with mushrooms, and Baz would be the man to do it with.

At the time of writing, Poppy is pregnant with her second child. A whole gamut of Goddesses, Angels, and a bossy harem-trousered wise woman surround her, all gathered around to oversee the incubation and birth of a brand new 'starseed'. She told me she worries we won't want to be friends with her because she's pregnant and can't take Mandy for a while, which isn't the case at all. It just goes to show that everyone has similar insecurities. They are true friends and we love them both dearly.

Melanie tells me to push myself forward more as she does, to invite myself to people's houses, and to suggest meetups instead of waiting to be invited. It seems to work for her and Robin, but Josh and I have had limited success with this approach. I do invite people, but there are only so many times you can do that without coming across as needy or being a downright pest (as in, "I don't want to come, get the message, will ya?").

I encouraged Josh to follow Melanie's advice with a nice guy we met at the camp called Matt. He was there with his wife Judy, and we got on well. Melanie suggested that Josh message him and ask if they could get together and jam on the guitar. Now, this is so out of Josh's comfort zone, but he did. Matt responded that yes, he'd like to do that, but he had work going on and he'd sort something out soon. Weeks passed, and I nagged Josh to message again, asking how Matt was and if he'd still like to meet up. He didn't receive a reply. Josh was feeling a bit upset, and I was sad and annoyed at myself for pushing him.

When I mentioned it to Melanie, she said: "Oh no, tell Josh not to message him as he's got some mental health stuff going on."

This is the problem: push and you're a pest because you do not know what's going on with people, or it may be that they simply don't want to see you. If you don't push, they might think you don't want to see *them*. Either way, for someone who isn't confident like Josh, it can be crushing. The thing is, we saw Matt a few times later at get-togethers and he and Josh got on great, but what works for Melanie left Josh with even less confidence for a while. Once we realised these things take time, we made more headway. Around a month later, Matt messaged Josh out of the blue, saying he'd had a tough few weeks. He and Josh chatted for a while and ended up arranging for us all to go see a band together.

Friendship needs to grow organically, like it did with Baz and Poppy, but it's hard to start the process if you don't get the opportunity to meet people who are also looking for friendship. The internet, particularly Facebook group comments, would have us believe that there are millions of people out there wishing they had a close friend. They are, however, extremely hard to find. Most people either already have an established group comprising family and long-term friends/acquaintances, or simply don't have the time or inclination to foster new friendships. I guess that's just life.

Around three years ago, I joined a guitar beginner's class. Sue, who taught the class, was just my kind of person. Very alternative in appearance, she wore long hippy skirts and had dreadlocks. The problem was that all the other beginners were of pensionable age. There was nothing wrong with that, but it wasn't the group I was looking for. After a while, I left, but Sue was on Facebook, which was where the classes were advertised. Her partner Steve is a DJ at psytrance events (psychedelic trance music). I like this kind of music for DMT trips. Melanie suggested that Josh and I take a pill and just go out and just talk to people to find others like us. I'm Melanie's mum foremost, and although she's my friend, I'm not her 'mate'. It wouldn't be healthy for her or me if I expected to be invited along to every social occasion. She and Robin have shown us the way, and we need to let go of their hands and take steps of our own. So Josh and I figured we'd take Melanie's advice. Still not sure about going out on Mandy together, Josh messaged DJ Steve. Within three messages, beginning with us asking for a list of events, Sue and Steve invited us to theirs for the evening for a meal. Also, we're booked in at a psytrance event later in the year, where Mandy is common but is not the major theme. Hopefully, we'll meet a whole new community of people.

I have pushed myself out there, sent invites, smiled. I've trusted strangers way too quickly, and often been over-generous, resulting in being taken advantage of. It's an ongoing thing for me. Maybe I had been asking too much from people and I didn't understand how to just go with the flow. Perhaps it's simply my age. After all, most people in their fifties and sixties are more like Mrs Cartwright next door. The important thing is that I'm open, and because I keep trying, I'm finding that things do just happen.

My children love me and have grown to trust me to be the person I should be. The most humbling thing is that they just want me to be happy. They invest their own time and their own families into making me feel whole, loved, and content. Melanie now tells me I'm the full package – funny, sexy, kind, and smart.

She also says, "Putting out someone else's flame doesn't make yours burn any brighter."

She's right, but it took me a long time to see that I didn't have to put someone else down to feel good about myself. Now that I understand people more, I make the effort to make others feel good about themselves. In fact, it's not even an effort.

I still have periods (for example after Christmas) when I feel down and sad that events are over. My mind tells me that nothing will be planned ever again, I won't be invited anywhere, I have no genuine friends, and there will be no more gatherings, and I feel sad. I went through it this year; I also went through it last year. I'm sure it will happen next year too. During these periods, I read self-help books on anxiety and enlightenment, but these feelings are so ingrained in me that I think I will always feel that way. Interestingly, more and more often, I hear that others are like me and feel the same anxieties. When I have these rocky moments, I try hard to fight them as I'm aware they are just the doubts my sober mind (as in Mandy free) nags me with. I find now that when I meet someone new, within a few conversations, I slide into the subject of drugs, either by mentioning raves or in a less obvious way by relating a story about a third party who takes recreational drugs. Then I gauge their reaction. Having said that, how would my pre-Mandy self have reacted to such a conversation? Probably in the same way we had initially reacted to Van Gav et al.

Gav is now one of the first people on our camp invites. He's a quiet, classy guy and good company, and it seems ridiculous and shameful that we judged him only as a threat to our normality. We heard his friend Lee got a job as a traffic warden, and we haven't seen him since that time we were in Melanie and Robin's living room.

There was an issue of friendships and the Mandy dynamic when Josh and I went over to Baz and Poppy's for the evening one weekend before Poppy fell pregnant. Unlike previously, they had asked us if we minded another couple joining us. We had met the woman before, as she was part of a spiritual group run by Baz. The man was a friend on Facebook who we hadn't met yet, so it seemed a good idea. 'Let's make more like-minded mates and all that.' It didn't quite work out that way.

The following day, we were due at a Christmas party with Melanie, Robin, and some other family, so we wanted to feel okay in the morning. I decided therefore to have a pill of 2CB instead of my usual Mandy. I had read that 2CB is a mix like that of MDMA and LSD. This mix results in a Mandy-type high with pleasant visuals, and virtually no come-down the day after, which sounded like a real bonus.

When we arrived, the woman, Chrissy, was already there, and the other guy, Neil, was coming later in the evening. We were providing the drugs, so we handed out the Mandy, I took my 2CB, and settled in for a fun evening. Within an hour, I wanted to go home. Josh and Baz were happily lounging on floor cushions and chatting away, and Poppy was cuddled up to Chrissy, having a deep conversation about the Universe. The group dynamic felt all wrong. The Mandy in the 2CB wasn't enough to allow me to join in. I felt anxious and excluded. I wasn't part of the girl talk or part of the guy talk. The level of psychedelics wasn't enough to affect me at all, except to make me feel disconnected and lacking in stimulation. I found myself randomly half dancing and half frantically wandering about their living room while they talked around me. This feeling would last all evening. When Neil turned up, he joined the guys talking, and I sat around like a spare part. It got to the point where I was begging Chrissy and Poppy, "Please talk to me!"

I had never felt that way before; like the LSD I had with Charlotte it hadn't been particularly strong, but the drug in me was seeking visual and social stimuli, making me feel isolated and edgy. Josh reckoned that had there been just the usual four of us, or another person to break the couples' thing up, it would have been alright. On the upside, Josh gets on very well with 2CB. In contrast to his experiences with Mandy, he stays awake and present in the conversation all evening and doesn't fall asleep in a corner, being forgotten about while I flutter around all and sundry talking rubbish and feeling the love all night.

I did try 2CB again a couple of weeks later, at a house party with over twenty-five people. Although I danced, chatted, and had a great time, I again didn't feel the level of ease and ability to let go that Mandy gives me. I was always very aware of my surroundings, but it felt more like mild paranoia. I imagined it must be like being the only teetotaller at a brewery works do. I couldn't get myself to relax. Many, many people love 2CB and have a fantastic time on it, Josh being one of them. However, I much prefer the full Mandy experience instead.

COVID changed people, but perhaps not as the media would have anticipated, and certainly not as they had reported it. On social media, a flood of groups has appeared over the last eighteen months, focused on spirituality and enlightenment. Once disparagingly labelled as hippies, they have hundreds of thousands of members, both locally and worldwide, still growing in numbers every day. People changed their outlook and took up hobbies. They gardened, foraged, and looked to reasons outside social construction for the state of the planet. The influence and power behind the messages of these new thinkers is increasing daily. With the addition of Mandy into the mix, my outlook on life changed, too. Even the trip to the

Buddhist temple, and the acknowledgement that I needed to look after myself mentally, hadn't been enough to change my feelings of burnout.

A few years ago, the company I worked for had been the subject of a takeover. The company that bought us out was notorious for the way they would treat employees as disposable numbers, not people. After working from home for almost twelve months, they introduced new systems to replace the ones we had used for over twelve years. They told us we were to take calls from customers immediately, from home, with no prior training. When the majority of employees complained about this, we were told to 'just muddle through'. I emailed the creator of the system to ask how it worked, and I sent daily emails to my boss to ask for training. I received nothing back. Josh was under considerable strain as he tried to help me, but with no knowledge of our systems, he could only watch as I got more and more upset. It wasn't fair to him, either.

Waking up one Monday morning, yet again feeling anxious with chest pains and dizziness, I couldn't log on to my work laptop. I was frozen in place, my head aching and foggy from lack of sleep. The systems buffered, lagged, and crashed mid-use. Every call to our tech support resulted in either no reply or a recorded message informing us to keep trying. After a month of being shouted and sworn at by customers, and the incredible stress of knowing nothing about a job at which I was previously a top performer, I felt utterly broken. My self-esteem was shot to pieces and my mental health was suffering to the extent that I had constant vertigo and two panic attacks in a week. As colleagues could not help each other, every internal message popping up, every conversation, and every email doing the rounds was full of despair, anger, and stress. People were at the end of their tether, and the depression and hopelessness spread like waves over a sinking ship.

My manager messaged me as I sat, just staring at the computer screen one morning after another sleepless night.

"Hi, Helen, are you still having trouble with the systems?"

I couldn't believe what I was hearing. What was he saying? Had he not been taking the slightest bit of notice for the past month?

"Can I call you?" he asked.

For the first time, I said exactly what I was feeling.

"No. I don't want to talk to you. I've tried and tried, and I just can't do it. Leave me alone," I replied flatly, ending the call.

I just didn't care any longer about what he thought. I didn't care about anything at that point. I felt no emotion whatsoever. He called again, of course, and I reiterated what the issues were, telling him just how low and helpless I was feeling.

"Take a day off and see how you feel after the weekend."

He made no inference that he would investigate the situation or that any training would be offered – just a useless day off.

I never logged on or worked for the company again. I could no longer work in an environment where I was simply a commodity, or where there was no consideration for my mental welfare. It was indicative of the company's attitude when a woman from Occupational Health called me some weeks later. I explained how I had been at the top of my role for over eighteen years, but I no longer felt I knew my job due to a total lack of support and training from the company. I poured out my frustration and concerns for both myself and the department as a whole.

"You know, I feel that you're something of a perfectionist," she murmured in a voice like warming syrup. She was so condescending that I almost exploded. I wasn't about to be made to feel small by anyone again.

"No," I answered firmly, "I'm a human being who has given the company one hundred per cent for eighteen years, and I've been pushed to the limit and crushed by them. I have never had a sick note in those eighteen years, and you're telling me now that the reason I can't cope is that I'm a perfectionist?"

Josh and I discussed, calculated, and ultimately decided that I could not go back to that situation. Within a month, with Josh's invaluable help, I started a dog walking and grooming business. It's not as easy as it sounds – some dogs are just nightmares, the owners can be worse and I'm constantly racing off to pick up dogs, feeling like I'm meeting myself coming back. I sweat and roast half the year and freeze and drown for the other, but life is good. I now earn my money working with animals, in the village I love, in the fields and woodlands I continue to learn so much from, and which soothe my heart – well, that's still a trifle too twee and not entirely accurate. The dogs are total dicks, but I love them all. They scarper off in all directions once let off their leads, and I've put my fingernails through more steaming bags of dog poo than I care to think about without gagging. I'm constantly covered in dog hair and my car looks like a leaking old barn find, complete with leaves and ripped-up seats.

My wage is no longer certain, and we have had to accept that we need to be a little more careful about what we spend, but the peace of mind for Josh and me is worth it. The last I heard, there were twelve of my old team of twenty workmates who were off on long-term sick with work-related stress, and *still,* there is no training or support from the company in the pipeline.

After worrying about relying on others, Josh got very brave and sourced some decent ecstasy pills in case Robin couldn't get any. Like the Salvia, we sent the money to some random seller on a random group on the internet with a username something like 'Inotscamubuymidrugz' and waited for the police. It was refreshing and surprising indeed when, instead of a uniformed henchman shaking his head and rattling his handcuffs at us, we got the plain brown envelope containing our stash – first-class post, no less! The goodies came wrapped in an air-sealed bag, then a cardboard sleeve, cling film around the card, then bubble wrap taped around that. This was quality control at its best! We had also added a couple more tabs of LSD to our order as a special treat, too.

We have made a couple more orders since then and Robin has also used the seller, so we've dropped lucky. Yes, it may be illegal, but it's also someone's business, so it pays them to be a reliable source. It's honest and safe to say that it's not become our whole lives by any means, but it's now an occasional and very enjoyable part. One aspect of our Mandy use is that Josh and I have done things, visited places, and met people we would never have done had it not been for Mandy.

A short while ago we both had a night out on Manchester's infamous Canal Street in the Gay Village. Melanie, Robin, Ally, and her new boyfriend joined us (the beautiful 'elf guy' from the rave who we now know as Justin). Anxious in large groups, we were both nervous about the evening ahead, so took a pill each before going out. The diverse groups of gay, trans, lesbian, and heterosexual people were enveloped in bright lights and colour, and we loved them all. We hugged with Mandy, we danced with Mandy, we chatted with strangers with Mandy, and we had no fear or judgement when Mandy was with us. We had booked an apartment for us all and once the pubs and clubs closed, we headed back to chat and listen to some ambient trance music. Of course, we didn't head to bed until almost dawn, but that's Mandy for you. It was a truly amazing experience.

It was a few days until I turned sixty. This shuffle dancing business was a lot harder than I had first imagined. I don't think my rough kitchen floor or aching feet from dog walking was helping my progress, but I practised whenever I could. Melanie was sending me regular video updates of how she was doing, and I was getting more and more despondent.

"Hiiiii!" Another video arrived. "Watch this!"

She was very, very good. Her rhythm and passion for the music were evident in her performance, and I was impressed by how far she'd come in such a short time.

"How are you doing with it?"

"Not bad," I lied. "My Running Man is okay."

It wasn't – it was awful. To Melanie's credit and my relief, she never asked for video proof of my dancing prowess, but I knew for sure that the anticipated couple's dance was never going to happen.

Thanks to my lovely family, I didn't wake up too depressed on the day of my birthday, but it soon became evident that I wouldn't be seeing Melanie at all. She had come down with a bug that had floored her. She sounded so poorly when she rang to wish me a happy birthday. I tried hard to hold back tears of disappointment, so I told her to snuggle up warm, said that it was fine, and to just get better.

Charlotte and Adz had arranged for us to go for a posh meal out that evening. Carl and his family had arranged to pop over to see me the next day. Josh did give me a heads-up that the restaurant was a very classy establishment, so I spent most of the day alternating between anxiety about what to wear and sadness at not seeing Melanie on my big day. At three o'clock, I called Charlotte.

"Charlotte, I have no idea what to wear! I don't have anything you'd call classy; my clothes are mainly hippie stuff!" I was stressed to death by then. "Can't you come down and see what you think? I'm worried I'm going to look like a right mess."

"Mum… Mum… Mum! Stop panicking!"

Charlotte calmly but firmly agreed to come to mine, do my hair, and then go back and get herself ready, bless her. Between us, I was wrestled into a short wine-coloured party dress, and Charlotte created the most amazing up-do with my hair. Once I'd got my makeup on, I felt like the proverbial million dollars and was starting to look forward to the meal.

It was nearly time to leave, and I was staggering around the kitchen in a pair of towering six-inch heels I hadn't dared to wear since I was forty. Josh, all dressed up and looking extremely handsome, was picking up the car keys when his phone rang. It was Charlotte. They had arrived a bit too early in town and asked if we could meet for a drink before going on to the restaurant. Her suggestion made sense, and it would be nice to have a quick natter beforehand.

We met in a town centre pub, which often had bands playing on a weekend. I'd been a few times before, so felt comfortable there – if a tad overdressed. I was also starving by this time, so hoped we wouldn't be there too long. In my wobbly heels, I teetered and sashayed up the stairs to the bar. Josh was behind me, with arms outstretched and hands cupped, ready to support my backside if I tripped (in the manner he had perfected last winter, when the mysterious naked lady appeared in our garden).

I could smell food. Opening the bar door, I said to Josh, "Something smells gorgeous; I'm starv—"

"SURPRISE!"

The assault of lights, yells of welcome, laughter, party-poppers, balloons, and people – so many people; hit me like a punch in the chest. I staggered with shock as I faced the room. I can only confirm that surprise parties you see on YouTube and social media are nothing like how you feel at the time. All these smiling faces… so much noise! *Who are all these people? I don't know this many people!*

Grandchildren came rushing over to hug my legs. As I leaned in to pull them toward me, I began to pick out individual faces in the crowd. Carl and Charlotte were there – grinning and teary with joy, wonderful Dawn who hated parties and felt out of place because of her deafness, lovely Baz and Poppy with their small daughter Meadow, a small group from my old job, and a neighbour from my past life with Adrian (a widow, she knew no one and had come alone). There were over sixty people, and all these people were there for me. Still shaking, I hugged each one of them in turn. Many of these people I wouldn't have met if it hadn't been for Mandy. Every single guest was precious to me in some way. And there she was – Melanie. *She made it!*

I can barely begin to describe the wonderful evening it was. Josh had arranged for my favourite local band to play, and I danced and laughed more than I had in years, with love and happiness that everyone had done something so special for me. Adrian was the DJ for the evening, playing a mix of all my favourite songs that Melanie had thoughtfully compiled in advance. I still have the playlist on my phone.

I smiled wryly to myself when Poppy came forward, carrying a heavily iced and glorious weed cake. As she plonked it down next to the buffet sandwiches, the aroma wafted and spread into the surrounding quiches and mini pork pies, to put smiles on faces ten feet away. This, however, was not the dessert that invited the most attention. The real star of the show was the birthday cake.

Pride of place, in the middle of the spread, was the most beautiful birthday cake you could imagine. Made up of three tiers, it was decorated with flowers, peace signs, and brightly coloured icing, which spelt 'Happy Birthday Helen.' Right on top was a VW hippie camper van made of chocolate cake and royal icing. It was a masterpiece of cake making. Mary Berry would have deemed herself not worthy of this glorious work of art. I looked closer, admiring the intricate petals of the daisies around the middle tier. *But what do those big white circles have iced on them?* I froze momentarily, eyes widening in shock as I read the lettering. I beckoned urgently to Carl (who had ordered the cake). He was happily chatting away to the huddle of people now taking photos of it.

"Carl, come here!" I hissed through the music and chatter. "Those discs on the cake have MDMA iced on them!"

Carl grinned back at me.

"There's a funny story behind that, Mum," he said, pulling me slightly to one side. "As a bit of an inside joke, I thought I'd ask the baker to put the chemical symbol for MDMA on the cake. I knew no one would know what it was except the people who do know, and that it would make you laugh."

I couldn't imagine where Carl was going with this story. Chuckling to himself at the memory, he explained further.

"When we picked the cake up this afternoon, it was in the box and looked amazing. Before you arrived, we set up all the food and left a space in the middle of the table for the cake. When I opened it, I was like, 'Oh my fucking God!'"

The baker had put the chemical symbol on an iced disc, but she'd also written MDMA underneath in icing too! *Oh shit.*

"I swear, Mum, that wasn't what I'd sent her. I'd only sent a drawing of the symbol."

The sudden flashes of camera phones momentarily distracted me. It was as if Elvis had burst from the sponge and frosting in full regalia, singing Jailhouse Rock.

"So why didn't she do what you'd asked for?" I muttered anxiously, watching the guests pointing at the cake. Never mind 'If you know, you know' the grinning faces and number of photos being taken appeared to be in direct proportion to how many people *did* know! I could imagine that Carl's artistic talents were probably more Picasso than Constable, but even so.

"Well, this woman's good at cake decorating and she thought she could find a better picture, so she got one online. Trouble is, the one she found said MDMA underneath, so she iced the whole thing."

Neither of us had time to continue the conversation as the party carried on around us. I took to the stage for a few moments to make a short speech. I wanted to tell the sea of faces just how much them being there meant to me. Every single one of them was a gift beyond price.

☺ ☺ ☺

The next day, standing in my kitchen with a cuppa, I found out the rest of the story from Melanie.

"So, Carl called me in a right panic before your party. He told me about what the baker had done so I suggested he try to scrape the letters off. He said he'd already tried, but it was ruining the icing. He'd tried removing the disc, but it left a big hole where it had been, so they had to stick it back on with jam."

I was wheezing with helpless and silent laughter at their predicament, which, obviously, I had known nothing about.

"I told him to just turn the cake around instead, so no guests would see the incriminating section."

Melanie and I were both bent double with mirth at the mental imagery.

"There was quiet for a moment, and I could hear Carl and Jemma fiddling around with the box, then suddenly, Carl shouted, 'Oh my God! There are another five discs! They're all around the cake! What are we gonna do?'"

They did what anyone would do in that predicament – they gave up. The cake went on display and became the talking point of the evening. I still have the little campervan cake topper and one of the MDMA discs in my freezer now.

The dilemma with the cake was only one of the countless stories from behind the scenes of surprise party planning. Josh had kept it secret for months as he organised, invited, researched venues, booked the band, and made loads of arrangements with Carl, Melanie, and Charlotte. I never got a sniff of anything going on. Each one of them contributed equally and gave their time over many weeks to ensure it was everything I could have dreamed of. The work and love involved still makes me feel humbled – I felt so special. I didn't know at the time, but Melanie had spent the whole day in tears because she was poorly and felt devastated she wouldn't be there for me until Charlotte called her with some words of wisdom.

"Melanie, you HAVE to be there. Take whatever medicine you need to feel half-alive and get to the party. If you don't come, Mum won't remember how wonderful the night was; all she'll remember is that you weren't there."

Poor Robin had been even more poorly than Melanie, and couldn't even get out of bed, never mind attend. He was so upset he couldn't make it.

The food hadn't been ready when they went to collect it, the balloons had to be blown up individually, but somebody had forgotten to bring the pump, all sixty balloons were inflated by sweating, purple-faced guests on the verge of collapse, moments before my arrival. After the event, I asked to see the guest list of who was invited and who did and didn't come. Some had wanted to be there but had valid reasons why they couldn't attend. My parents were invited but with my dad so frail, I understood why they didn't come. Mind you, my mum hadn't shown up at Katy's fiftieth ten years ago either, so Dad went alone. Two of my male friends from many years ago had promised to come. They had been invited because they were both a very special part of my past. One was from when I was a teenager, and the other was a platonic friend throughout my twenties and thirties. The latter friend was like the brother I never had when I was married to Adrian. They were told just how much it would mean to me to see them again, and they both, right until the last minute, agreed to come. Neither turned up. One of them confirmed he would be coming with his family the day before, and then, without a word, simply didn't bother. He lives less than five minutes from the venue.

One invaluable lesson I learned that night was to let go of one-sided emotional attachments. I could have been upset, but instead, I realised that I was more attached to the memory of them than they were to me. That acceptance brought me emotional freedom and I doubt I will think of either of them again. The ones that mattered were there. Josh had invited anyone and everyone he thought might turn up. The trio from work turned up for a nosey. I'd been off work for over a year. There was free food and a band and without being ungrateful, I know that's why they came. Put it this way, I contacted all three to thank them for coming and suggested we meet again for a drink in the future, and not one of them replied. Interestingly, out of the guests who were invited and did turn up, the majority were people I had met either because of or since meeting Mandy.

Recreational drugs aren't for everyone. Of course, I must state the obvious – there is a risk with anything we put into our bodies. I cannot make that call for anyone else but myself. Drugs on their own can't solve anyone's problems, nor have they solved mine – they have just shown me another way, another perspective. The war on drugs will never be won. It has only driven them further underground, thus spawning unscrupulous manufacturers and dealers. These people take risks with the health of their customers as the raw ingredients become harder to obtain. Sadly, it has also meant that people who could benefit from the therapy they can offer are currently denied that option.

The choices are, as always, down to us as individuals, but what I have learned for myself is to know my source as best I can. With DMT, it's safer and more accessible to extract our own. Similarly, with mushrooms, if I pick my own, then I know my source. I always watch my dosage and don't let anyone push me to take more. I'm now more able to talk about my problems, but equally, I don't feel the need to share them every time I have Mandy. I don't take Mandy every time I see people. If it's too late in the day or I'm not in the mood, I can take it or leave it. If I do have Mandy or DMT, I only have them in the company of people I trust, and I make sure I drink plenty of water.

I'm also mindful of Melanie's advice about oversharing and getting overwhelmed by the hedonistic vibe often associated with MDMA use. In our case, Josh and I have found that as a couple, there is more awareness of the balance of permissions allowed in connections with others. A lot of hugging and cuddling goes on, but everyone has their line in the sand over which regrets, and embarrassment lie.

Mandy releases people from their inhibitions. 'She' released Josh and me from ours so that we could relax and have fun with strangers, but equally, Mandy has no idea what you may call fun and simply lets you decide in the moment. At the time, it feels like everyone is a friend for life – a soulmate. Maybe this might be true on a rare occasion, but more often it is what it is – just a lovely connection with like-minded humans for the evening.

At the start of my journey, I was afraid the connections made would peter out, but Josh and I haven't found that to be the case. People are still people and sharing one evening with Mandy doesn't mean that we'll share interests in the morning, but in a few cases, it has. I found that most people I met I liked, as they had the happy-go-lucky but ultimately responsible lives that Josh and I had. It's a fallacy that all recreational drug users are unemployed losers. On the contrary, I haven't met one yet that would fall into that category. Even if I had, I would be far less likely to judge. The people I have stayed in touch with and met outside a camp or event are few, but are now our Mandy 'family'. I've learned it's fine and normal to be hugging a stranger all evening, but in the morning realise they weren't your kind of person after all. Mandy opens the way for introductions. It doesn't make future plans for you. I've learned that a good get-together is a careful balance between social relaxation and common sense.

There would always be at least one 'happy chappy' who would genuinely just want everyone to have a great time. They would often periodically appear with another 'dab' or half a pill, just to keep the happy vibe and the 'coming up' roll going. The dabs would often be in the drinks that were offered, which I wasn't always aware of at the time of accepting them.

Quickly I realised that one pill, then maybe a quarter/half a pill two hours later, is enough for me. If I have a bottle of water handy, I'm not tempted to accept the random drinks handed around. I made that decision after a house party where

I had pills, dabs, weed to come down with, and explosive vomiting. I felt terrible upon waking, and it was enough to make me take up the reins again and party responsibly.

Since my first ever ecstasy tablet, I have closely followed the progress of trials for MDMA in therapeutic settings. I say with conviction that I believe it's a wonder drug. I do still suffer from anxiety, which probably relates to my old work situation, but I manage this by changing my physical environment, recognising my triggers, and using natural remedies, as well as the occasional synthetic kind, of course! Being menopausal, I'm aware a lot of my generalised anxiety is based on my fear of having a lot more years behind me now than I have ahead. This is something I can only really talk to my sister Katy about, as she has the same worries. Melanie can't yet relate, and I don't want to project my worries onto her. Josh listens but being male, his understanding is limited. I believe it's completely natural to feel this way, and I don't see it as a flaw in my character that I worry about my mortality at this stage in my life, but my experiences with DMT have helped. I try to focus on my emotional well-being as much as possible.

LSD and Psilocybin *can* aggravate symptoms of depression and anxiety in some cases. Equally, there is an abundance of supportive evidence that they can also alleviate depression, and research into this is currently ongoing. The magnitude of how my life has changed since that first introduction to Mandy escapes even me sometimes. How I summoned up the courage to deconstruct my past, dissect my personality, and leave the security of the longest employment I have ever had, all in a couple of years, is mind-boggling, but I hope it will be inspiring to others.

The other day, I was watching TV with my eleven-year-old grandson Ethan. There was a scene in the movie with some drunk people falling over and shouting angrily at one another.

"You know what I'd do, Granny? I'd invent a pill. I'd call it 'Happy', or 'Joy', and when people took it, they'd be happy. They wouldn't fight or be angry, and everyone would like their jobs."

I looked at him, musing for a moment, and nodded.

"Yeah, I think that's called drugs, Ethan, and they're illegal."

I pondered the simplicity of both his statement and my response.

"I know, Granny," he replied, "and that's why the world is stupid. How can happiness be illegal?"

THE END

Note from the Author

Thank you for taking the time to read my book. I hope it gave you a few laughs and maybe even opened your mind a little to how even the most bizarre of opportunities can change your path forever.

If you enjoyed the book, I would be so grateful if you would leave a review because that is how we poor and unknown writers get our kicks; from knowing we made someone happy for a while.

Please feel free to contact me using the methods below – I'd love to hear from you!

Email: info@helen-brennan.com
Web: https://www.helen-brennan.com
Facebook: https://www.facebook.com/helenbrennanauthor

If any of the topics raised in this book have hit a bit close to home and you need help, I am adding a few links so you can get help.

Refuge (Domestic Abuse Support)
https://www.nationaldahelpline.org.uk/

Mind (Mental Health Support)
https://www.mind.org.uk/

Frank (Drug Support)
https://www.talktofrank.com/

NHS (Loneliness Support)
https://www.nhs.uk/mental-health/feelings-symptoms-behaviours/feelings-and-symptoms/feeling-lonely/

Printed in Great Britain
by Amazon

22130267R00159